ISBN 978-0-266-01931-2
PIBN 10960602

This book is a reproduction of an important historical work. Forgotten Books uses
state-of-the-art technology to digitally reconstruct the work, preserving the original format
whilst repairing imperfections present in the aged copy. In rare cases, an imperfection in
the original, such as a blemish or missing page, may be replicated in our edition. We do,
however, repair the vast majority of imperfections successfully; any imperfections that
remain are intentionally left to preserve the state of such historical works.

ve Document

content reflects current
edge, policies, or practices.

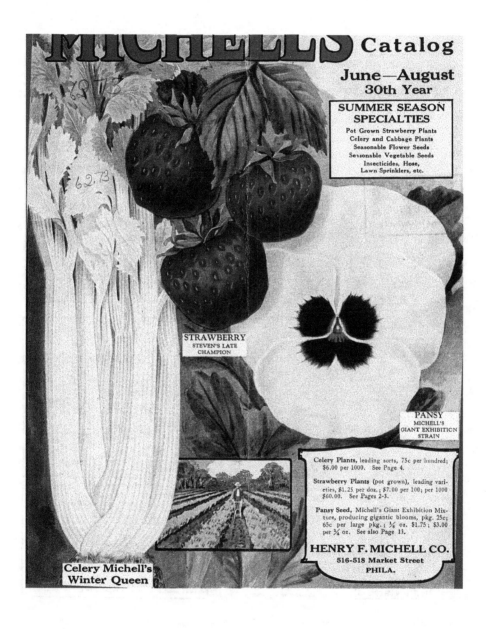

MICHELLS Catalog

June—August
30th Year

STRAWBERRY
STEVEN'S LATE
CHAMPION

PANSY
MICHELL'S
GIANT EXHIBITION
STRAIN

Celery Michell's
Winter Queen

Celery Plants, leading sorts, 75c per hundred; $6.00 per 1000. See Page 4.

Strawberry Plants (pot grown), leading varieties, $1.25 per doz.; $7.00 per 100; per 1000 $60.00. See Pages 2-3.

Pansy Seed, Michell's Giant Exhibition Mixture, producing gigantic blooms, pkg. 25c; 65c per large pkg.; ⅛ oz. $1.75; $3.00 per ¼ oz. See also Page 13.

HENRY F. MICHELL CO.
516-518 Market Street
PHILA.

U. S. FOOD ADMINISTRATION License G. 36797

BUSINESS TERMS

When sending your first charge order, if possible, send us the name and address of someone with whom you already have a charge account. This saves time.

NOTICE TO CUSTOMERS OUTSIDE OF THE UNITED STATES

In remitting for purchases at the time of ordering or when paying accounts, by reason of the exchange, we ask that you please send P. O. Money Order in U. S. funds or a check or draft on a New York or Phila. Bank in par U. S. funds.

REGARDS C. O. D. SHIPMENTS

Goods can be sent C. O. D. (with the exception of perishable items, which include plants and cold - storage bulbs; these cannot be sent C. O. D.). No C. O. D. shipments for any kind of goods can be made by express or freight out of town unless a partial remittance accompanies the order. No C. O. D. orders where the amount is less than 50c., except in the following zone in Philadelphia: Market Street Ferry, to Sixteenth Street, Pine Street, to Vine Street C. O. D. orders outside of this zone in our delivery limits must amount to $1.00 or more. During April no orders C. O. D. in their entirety can be accepted.

SHIPPING INSTRUCTIONS

Always state by what method you want goods forwarded, otherwise we will ship according to our best judgment.

PACKING CHARGES

No charge is made for boxes, packing or bags, except for two-bushel seamless sacks, which are returnable for credit at the market price as charged.

PARCEL POST SHIPMENT AT OUR EXPENSE AS FOLLOWS

We pay postage charges on all orders for vegetable and flower seeds, provided the order calls for packets, ounces, quarter-pounds and pounds (beans, corn, peas and mixed grass seeds, bulbs, plants and sundries are not included). If these are wanted by mail, remit for postage according to rate of postage from Philadelphia to your post office.

Parcels Post weight limits are 70 lbs. in 1st, 2d and 3d zone; in all other zones 50 lbs.

Bird's Eye View
MICHELL'S NURSERIES and GREENHOUSES
Andalusia, Penna.

HENRY F. MICHELL CO.

HENRY F. MICHELL, PRES.   FRED'K. J. MICHELL, VICE PRES.

SALESROOMS, OFFICES } 516-518 MARKET ST., PHILADELPHIA
ORDER DEPARTMENTS

Warehouses: 509-511-513 Ludlow Street, Philadelphia, Pa.

Garage 2114-16 Locust Street
Nurseries and Greenhouses, Andalusia, Pa.

Please address all communications and orders to
516-518 MARKET STREET, PHILA.

SPECIAL ATTENTION TO TELEPHONE ORDERS

BELL AND KEYSTONE
TELEPHONE CONNECTION

IMPORTANT NOTICE—PLEASE READ

Henry F. Michell Company give no warranty, expressed or implied, as to the description, purity or productiveness of any seeds, plants and bulbs they send out, and they cannot be in any way responsible for the crop. If the customer does not accept the goods on these terms, they can be returned at once and no sale has been made.

Prices are subject to any advances over present prevailing freight rates, customs duties or war tax, and all deliveries are subject to delay, restrictions, embargoes, crop shortages and all conditions beyond our control. All quotations are made and all orders are booked subject to the above conditions.

Merchandise to be credited must be returned within 5 days in good order free of expense to us.

Index to Contents of Michell's 1920 Summer Catalogue

MICHELL'S POT-GROWN STRAWBERRY PLANTS

EXTRA SELECTED STOCK—Strong and Well Rooted. Will Yield a Full Crop of Berries Next Season. Ready Now.

The time of shipment is from July 1st to September 15th. The advantages in planting pot-grown strawberry plants are realized by a full crop of berries the following year. Our plants are carefully grown in clay pots and prior to shipment are transferred with the original ball of earth at their roots to substantial paper pots in which they are forwarded, thus insuring the buyer getting them in first-class order and reducing the transportation charges about 25 per cent.

CULTURAL NOTE ON STRAWBERRIES

Strawberries delight in good rich soil that has had plenty of manure added to it. The plants should be set 12 to 15 inches apart in rows 2 feet apart. A row 100 feet long requires approximately 75 to 100 plants or about 14,500 per acre. If the weather is dry, when planting, water well at the time and for a few days thereafter, if it is possible. Press the soil well around the ball, when planting, and keep the soil well cultivated, cutting off all runners that may form. At the approach of permanent winter it pays to cover the entire bed to a depth of 2 inches with clean straw or salt hay. This protects the plants during severe weather. Do not use leaves, as they hold the moisture and cause damage to the plants in winter. At the approach of spring, rake the covering from the plants proper and leave it between the rows; this will serve as a mulch during the summer, protecting against drought, and also keeps the fruit more free from sand; at the same time to a large measure controls the growth of weeds.

EARLY VARIETIES

Early Jersey Giant (Perfect). Pre-eminently the finest of the early varieties. It is brilliant scarlet-crimson in color, and exceptionally firm, by far the firmest of all early sorts. Berries very large, conical with pointed tip; has delightful aroma and rich, mild strawbery flavor. A very heavy yielder.

Early Ozark (Perfect). Among the very first to ripen and the berries are of fairly good size; bright, crimson color; slightly conical; quite firm and of excellent quality. A strong grower and a heavy yielder.

Senator Dunlap (Perfect). This grand Strawberry will please the most critical person. One of the first to yield and continues well into the height of the season. It cannot be recommended too highly.

MID-SEASON VARIETIES

Big Joe (Perfect). The merits of this splendid variety are great vigor of plant, splendid root system, exceptional productiveness, large size of fruit, excellent flavor, and length of bearing season. The berries are perfect beauties, of very uniform, conical shape, rich red in color. In size the berries are not surpassed by those of any other variety grown, while the flavor is superior to that of most large fruited sorts. The plants root very deep, the roots going 10 to 12 inches in the ground, and they are but little influenced by droughts.

Brandywine (Perfect). The finest of all mid-season sorts; it has not a single defect. The plants are of extra strong constitution and growth, doing well everywhere. Fruit extra large, heart-shaped; color, bright, rich red.

Bubach (I). A fine old standard variety, especially popular in the middle and northern States. The blossoms are imperfect and must be planted with some perfect flowering variety in order that they may be pollenized, otherwise they will produce no fruit.

A husky developed specimen like this can't fail but give you satisfaction

MID-SEASON VARIETIES (Continued)

Glen Mary (Perfect). One of the best of the older varieties, as it still keeps its place among the prominent strawberries. The fruit is very large but rather irregular, somewhat like Sharpless. It is a great drought resister, ripening a full crop of luscious berries in the driest weather.

Heritage (Perfect). This is truly a giant strawberry, it being almost impossible to put a whole berry at a time in one's mouth. It is rather irregularly shaped but of a beautiful crimson color. The plants and foliage are entirely distinct which makes it stand out above all other sorts.

Rewastico (Perfect). The berries are a light cardinal red, uniformly large and regular in shape. The fruit is firm enough to carry to distant markets in good condition. The quality is extra fine. Blossoms are perfect and rich in pollen.

Price of Pot-grown Strawberries on this page $1.25 per dozen; per 100, $7.00; $60.00 per 1000.

NOTE—About October 1st we can furnish layer plants of any of the above varieties at 60c. per dozen; 25 for 75c.; $1.40 per 50; per 100, $2.50; $15.00 per 1000. If wanted by Parcel Post add 10c. per doz. or 20c. per 100 for postage. Larger quantities travel best by express.

Pot-grown Strawberry Plants can best be shipped by express.   No Plants sent C. O. D.   (oe)

MICHELL'S POT-GROWN STRAWBERRY PLANTS[3]

LATE SEASON VARIETIES

See Special Cultural
Note on Page 2

First Quality (Perfect). Berries are very large, pointed, and of a dark red color. Plants are very vigorous and healthy. Blossoms are perfect, strong pollenizers, making it a good variety to plant with imperfect varieties. A good variety for the home as well as for shipping purposes.

Gandy (Perfect). This variety is known to most every berry grower as one of the best late sorts. It is very solid and large, and of a beautiful crimson color; especially good for family garden planting.

Sharpless (Perfect). One of the old timers, but a variety of real merit; a tremendous cropper; plants very vigorous and hardy.

Stevens' Late Champion (Perfect). "Very large, fine flavored, bright color, good shipper, heavy yielder, good fruit stem." This berry has averaged 7556 quarts per acre, netting $666.96 per acre. It has been tested on all kinds of soils and will grow successfully where any strawberry will grow. It will stand a drought better than any other berry ever grown in this section. It has never shown any sign of rust.

Price of Pot-grown Late-Season Varieties Strawberries, $1.25 per dozen; per 100, $7.00; $60.00 per 1000.

NOTE—About October 1st we can furnish layer plants of any of the above varieties (except as noted) at 60c. per doz.; 25 for 75c.; $1.40 for 50; per 100, $2.50; $15.00 per 1000. If wanted by Parcel Post add 10c. per doz. or 20c. per 100 for postage.

Type of Everbearing Strawberries

MICHELL'S SPECIAL GRADE BONE MEAL

An excellent fertilizer to use when planting strawberries; about a teaspoonful to a plant. 25 lbs., $1.25; $2.25 per 50 lbs.; 100 lbs., $4.25; $8.00 per 200 lbs.

Stevens Late Champion

MICHELL'S AUTUMN FRUITING OR EVER-BEARING STRAWBERRY PLANTS

(Pot Grown)

This type, while producing its main crop of berries with the general sorts, continues uninterruptedly to mature its fruit, until checked by hard frosts; it has actually been known to bear strawberries until Christmas, when the weather is open and mild. In order to get the greatest crop of berries late, the blossoms should be kept cut off until August 1st, so as to conserve the energies of the plants for the fall crop. The plants must not be allowed to suffer for water in the fruiting season and a mulch of well rotted cow manure will be found of great advantage.

Peerless (New). This variety is claimed to be the best fall-bearing variety, producing right up to heavy frosts, as the fruit is protected by the large vigorous foliage.

Progressive. The berries are medium in size and delicious in quality. You can get fruit a few weeks after the plants are set and they continue to bear until freezing weather.

Superb. The fruit is large, firm and of fine quality. In addition to its value as a fall bearer, Superb will bear an excellent crop of berries in the spring. They look well and ship well.

Price of Everbearing Strawberry Plants (Pot-grown), $1.25 per dozen; per 100, $7.00; $60.00 per 1000. Layer Plants ready in October, 75c. per doz.; per 25, 85c.; $1.50 for 50; 100 for $2.75; $22.50 per 1000.

Pot-grown Strawberry Plants can best be shipped by express.   No Plants sent C. O. D.   (oe)

Extra Strong Celery Plants

(Ready About July 10)

A WORD ON CELERY CULTURE.—Celery delights in a good, rich, moist soil. Locations where the soil may become dry should be avoided. Nothing is more beneficial or so little work as the watering of celery during periods of drought. After it has been transplanted and made some growth, the plants should be set in permanent rows 6 to 8 inches apart in the row. Many private gardeners prefer to use the two-row system of trenches; it will be found very advantageous to work. If the idea of the market gardener is carried out, the celery is planted in single rows about 2 feet apart, 6 or 8 inches apart in the row. By the former method the celery is usually banked up to blanch until almost entirely covered with soil; the top is then covered with leaves or other litter as winter approaches. In the single-row system the celery is banked up gradually to blanch, and after this process is over, at the approach of winter it is dug up and laid in shallow trenches after being cleaned. Storing for winter is done by covering it with waterproof celery paper and topping off with soil or leaves. The celery may thus be gotten out for market during the severest weather. Good cultivation is highly necessary during the growing period.

French Golden Self-Blanching. An early sort. The heart is a rich golden-yellow, with light yellowish-green outer leaves.

Giant Pascal. One of the largest stalked kinds. It is in its prime for use during February and March, and can be used well up into spring.

White Plume. The White Plume is unsurpassed for fall and early winter use, requiring very little earthing to blanch it.

Winter Queen. This variety grows a very thick, solid and heavy stalk, and has a large heart. It is a close, compact grower, and when blanched is a creamy-white color.

Price of any of above Celery Plants, 75c. per 100; 500 for $3.25; $6.00 per 1000.

We cannot supply less than 50 celery plants of any one variety.

If wanted by Parcel Post allow 4 lbs. weight per 100 for postage.

Brussels Sprouts Plants

(Ready from July 1st to August 15th)

Matchless Improved. The plants should be well cultivated and kept free from insects. When heads begin to crowd, the lower leaves should be broken from the stem of the plant to give them plenty of room. 25 for 25c.; 75c. per 100; per 1000, $6.00.

If wanted by Parcel Post add 10c. per 100 for postage.

Perfection Drumhead Savoy Cabbage

CABBAGE PLANTS

Late Flat Dutch. A short stemmed, large, flat-headed variety; very solid; keeps the entire winter when buried in cellars or pits.

Red Dutch Drumhead. This cabbage is very sweet and should be used more largely. It is an excellent winter keeper.

Danish Ballhead. Unequaled for keeping qualities, massiveness and weight of heads.

Price of any of above Cabbage Plants, 25 for 25c.; 60c. per 100; per 1000, $4.00.

We cannot supply less than 25 cabbage plants of a variety. If wanted by Parcel Post add 15c. per 100 for postage.

THE BALL CELERY BLEACHER

A practical, inexpensive device for bleaching celery early, made of stiff, heavy paper. If the tubes are to be left on the plants all winter and the soil drawn around them, you get celery clean and sweet.

		Per 50	100	1000
No. 1.	6 x 12 in. Wt. Per 100, 8 lbs.	$1.50	$2.75	$21.00
No. 2.	6½ x 13 in. Wt. per 100, 10 lbs.	1.65	3.00	25.00
No. 3.	7 x 14 in. Wt. per 100, 14 lbs.	1.75	3.25	28.00

BALL CELERY HANDLER

Brass, $4.50 each. Tin, $1.75 each.

(oe)

MICHELL'S RELIABLE BULBS

FOR SUMMER AND EARLY AUTUMN PLANTING

Our General Bulb Catalog will be ready in September, and will contain a complete list of Bulbs for fall planting.

Easter in 1921 Comes on March 27th

AMARYLLIS

One of the most gorgeous showy house plants, giving splendid satisfaction, not only because of their requiring little care, but of their everlasting nature and tendency to increase.

Cultural Directions.—Place bulbs in live moss, only moderately moist, near window of a warm room. Watch the bulbs carefully, and when the first sign of growth appears through the top, get a six-inch pot and be ready to pot them up. The soil to be used should be fairly rich and when the bulb is set, most of it should be above the soil. Be moderate in watering first, but increase as growth increases, then place in a warm, light room near the window.

Belladonna. A beautiful bright pink. 40c. each; doz., $4.00; $30.00 per 100.

Formosissima. Crimson. 25c. each; per doz., $2.50; $17.50 per 100.

Johnsoni. Crimson, striped white. Large bulbs, 60c. each; doz., $6.00.

White Calla Lily

CALLA LILY BULBS
(Ready in September)

Callas require good, rich soil and plenty of warmth and water to make them thrive. Plant Callas indoors only.

GODFREY DWARF EVERBLOOMING CALLA (New)

This comparatively new calla has proven an excellent one; its character is exactly like the Æthiopica or regular variety, except it is of much dwarfer habit and freer bloomer; very desirable as a pot plant. Large blooming size bulbs, 25c. each; doz., $2.75; $17.50 per 100.

CALLA AETHIOPICA

	Each	Doz.	100
White, Monster Size, 2 to 2½ in. diam.....	$0.50	$5.00	$35.00
" Mammoth Size, 1¾ to 2 in. diam..	.30	3.00	20.00
" Medium Size, 1½ to 1¾ in. diam..	.20	2.00	12.50
" First Size, 1¼ to 1½ in. diam.....	.15	1.50	10.00
(Other varieties of Callas ready in October)			

Purity Freesia

FREESIA "PURITY"

This grand type supersedes all the old varieties of Freesias. The flowers are almost twice the size of the regular type; they also differ somewhat, being a pure glistening white; the stems are often 15 inches long and very wiry, rendering it a most valuable cut flower. Each bulb will produce 3 or 4 flower stems.

	Each	Doz.	100	1000
First Size Bulbs....................	$0.04	$0.35	$2.00	$17.50
Mammoth Size Bulbs...............	.05	.50	2.75	22.50
Monster Size Bulbs................	.08	.75	4.00	37.50
Jumbo Bulbs	.10	1.00	6.00	50.00

---

6 Bulbs of any one variety at dozen rate; 25 at 100 rate; 250 at 1000 rate.   (oe)

MICHELL'S RELIABLE BULBS

For Summer and Early Autumn Planting

FRENCH ROMAN HYACINTHS

(Ready in August)

French Roman Hyacinths afford a continuous supply of bloom from early winter until late in spring if planted in succession (two weeks apart). They are very fragrant.

They are easily grown in pots or pans. The bulbs, if potted in August or September, the pots plunged in the open ground for a month, until the bulbs are well rooted, and then brolght in the house, they can be had in flower in November or December, and a continuous supply of these delightful flowers may be had, by bringing in a few pots or pans of the rooted bulbs at intervals of about 2 weeks. The bulbs should be planted quite close together, a 6-inch pot or pan will be sufficiently large enough for six bulbs. They are not hardy and are not suitable for outdoor planting.

White, Extra select, size 12-15 cm.
" Mammoth, 13-15 cm.
" Monster, 15 cm. and over.
Light Pink
Light Blue
White Italian. Late; large spikes.

} Crop of these is uncertain; please write for prices.

Parcel post weight, 1 lb. per doz.; per 100, 8 lbs.

TESTIMONIAL ON MICHELL'S BULBS

Commissioners of Luzerne County
Wilkes-Barre, Pa.

The bulbs received from you last year were first-class in every way and gave results that were very much appreciated by the Commissioners as well as the public in general.

N. C. KEELY.

Court House, Wilkes-Barre, Pa.

Michell's Monster White Roman Hyacinths

Narcissus Paper White Grandiflora

MICHELL'S EARLY NARCISSUS

(Polyanthus Type) (Ready in August)

This class of Narcissus is a most interesting one. They may be grown in water and pebbles like Chinese lilies, but they are equally suited for growing in soil. The flowers are produced in clusters, like the illustration, and are delightfully fragrant. Not suitable for outdoors. Parcel Post Weight of Polyanthus Narcissus, 2 lbs. per doz.; per 100, 12 lbs.

Double Roman. White perianth, with an orange and yellow suffused cup, very free flowering and early. 5c. each; per doz., 50c.; $3.25 per 100; per 1000, $27.50.

Glorisa. A showy type, with white perianth and orange yellow cup. 10c. each; doz., 80c.; $4.50 per 100; per 1000, $40.00.

Grand Monarque. Large, broad, white perianth with a primrose-yellow cup; a very striking flower. 6c. each; per doz., 60c.; $4.00 per 100; per 1000, $32.50.

Grand Primo. Large white perianth with yellow cup. 8c. each; per doz., 85c.; $6.00 per 100; per 1000, $55.00.

Grand Soleil d'Or (often called "Yellow Paperwhite"). Rich yellow, with deep red cup. For cutting this is a fine variety. 10c. each; per doz., $1.00; $7.50 per 100.

Paper White Grandiflora, First Size Bulbs. This is quite a specialty with us; of it alone we import over two million bulbs. It is a pure white flowering sort; used extensively for forcing, as it can be brought into bloom in 8 weeks' time; the stems are very long and it is excellent for bunching. 6c. each; per doz., 60c.; $3.50 per 100; per 1000, $30.00.

Paper White Grandiflora, Mammoth Bulbs. 8c. each; per doz., 70c.; $4.50 per 100; per 1000, $40.00.

Paper White Grandiflora, Giant Bulbs. 10c. each; doz., $1.00; $6.00 per 100; per 1000, $50.00.

White Pearl. A large pure white; very exquisite. 10c. each; per doz., 85c.; $6.25 per 100; per 1000, $55.00.

(See page 7 for other Early Narcissus)

For Summer and Early Autumn Planting

MICHELL'S TRUMPET NARCISSUS
(For Early Forcing)

Extra Early Emperor. Excellent early variety for forcing; flowers are pure golden yellow. 10c. each; doz., $1.00; $6.50 per 100.

Extra Early Golden Spur. For Christmas and New Year's forcing this strain is far in the lead of the regular Dutch type. Free flowering, producing rich, golden yellow blooms, 10c. each; doz., $1.00; $6.50 per 100.

French Trumpet Major (Christmas Flowering). A beautiful early flowering yellow variety. They force easily and can be had in flower without any trouble for Christmas. 7c. each; doz., 65c.; $4.25 per 100; per 1000, $35.00.

Single Narcissus, French Trumpet Major

LILIUM HARRISH
(The Bermuda Easter Lily)

Cultural Note—In order to obtain best results, attention to the following brief directions will assist materially: Upon receiving the bulbs, pot them immediately. Place a handful of well-rotted cow manure in the bottom of the pot and place the bulb directly on top, covering it with soil. After watering, place in an outside pit and protect from the direct rays of the sun; cover well with soil, ashes or any other suitable litter. When the bulbs have become thoroughly rooted, bring inside, in a temperature of about 60 degrees; let the plants grow slowly under a bench or some other suitable place until about 6 inches high; then place on top of the bench. About two months before Easter they can be brought into a warmer temperature and gradually forced into flower and height at one time. An occasional application of liquid cow manure, starting about six weeks before flowering time, will stimulate the plant wonderfully. Thorough rooting is the most essential point.

MICHELL'S "SPECIAL BRAND" LILIUM HARRISH
(True Bermuda Easter Lily)

Noted for freedom from disease, uniformity and free flowering qualities.

	Each	Doz.	100
5 to 7 inches circum.	$0.30	$3.00	$22.50
6 to 7 " "	.50	5.00	35.00
7 to 9 " "	.60	6.00	45.00
9 to 11 " "	1.00	11.00	
11 to 13 " "	1.50	15.00	

LILIUM LONGIFLORUM MULTIFLORUM
MICHELL'S SPECIAL BRAND (Ready in October)

This brand must not be compared with lower priced bulbs, as it is a distinct selection.

P. P. Wt. per doz.	Each	Doz.	100
7 to 9 inches circum., 3½ lbs.	$0.40	$4.00	$30.00
8 to 10 inches circum., 4 lbs.	.60	6.00	45.00
9 to 10 inches circum., 5 lbs.	.75	8.00	60.00
Monster Bulbs 7 lbs.	1.00	10.00	

LILIUM FORMOSUM
(The Formosa Easter Lily)

Similar to the Bermuda Lily, but blooms earlier.
Dark Stemmed Type
(Flowering generally in March and April)

P. P. Wt. per doz.	Each	Doz.	100
7 to 9 inches circum., 3½ lbs.	$0.60	$6.00	$45.00
9 to 10 inches circum., 5 lbs.	.75	8.00	60.00
10 to 12 inches circum., 7 lbs.	1.00	10.00	
Monster Bulbs 9 lbs.	1.25	12.50	

Green Stemmed Type
(Flowering generally in January, February and March)

P. P. Wt. per doz.	Each	Doz.	100
6 to 8 inches circum., 2½ lbs.	$0.40	$4.00	$30.00
7 to 9 inches circum., 3½ lbs.	.60	6.00	45.00
9 to 10 inches circum., 5 lbs.	.75	8.00	60.00
10 to 12 inches circum., 7 lbs.	1.00	10.00	
Monster Bulbs 9 lbs.	1.25	12.50	

LILIUM LONGIFLORUM GIGANTEUM (True)

P. P. Wt. per doz.	Each	Doz.	100
6 to 8 inches, circum., 2½ lbs.	$0.40	$4.00	$30.00
7 to 9 inches circum., 3½ lbs.	.60	6.00	45.00
9 to 10 inches circum., 5, lbs.	.75	8.00	60.00
Monster Bulbs, 10 to 12 inches circum., 7 lbs.	1.25	12.50	

LILIUM LONGIFLORUM "AZORES"

A splendid strain, grown at the "Azores," producing strong, uniform flowers. Free from disease.

	Each	Doz.	100
6 to 7 inches circum.	$0.40	$4.00	$30.00
7 to 9 inches circum.	.60	6.00	45.00
9 to 11 inches circum.	1.00	11.00	

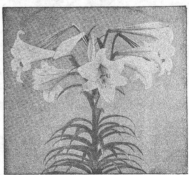

Lil. Giganteum

.6 Bulbs of a variety at dozen rate; 25 at 100 rate; 250 at 1000 rate (oe)

MICHELL'S RELIABLE BULBS
FOR SUMMER AND EARLY AUTUMN PLANTING

LILIUM CANDIDUM
(Madonna Lily)
(Ready in August)

This variety is sometimes called St. Joseph's, Madonna, or Annunciation Lily. One of the most popular and satisfactory of the American garden lilies. Pure waxy white flowers produced on straight stems bearing anywhere from 10 to 30 blooms of good size and substance; delightfully fragrant. Effective planting is the result of massing them in clumps or borders. Our bulbs are grown in Northern France, where they have a reputation of growing the finest in the world. To insure absolute success, plant the bulbs as early as possible—September preferred—6 inches deep, imbedded in sand and placed on their side; height, 4 feet; blooms in June.

	Each	Doz.	100
Large Bulbs....	$0.15	$1.50	$9.00
Mammoth Bulbs	.20	2.00	12.50
Monster Bulbs..	.25	2.50	17.50

Lilium Candidum (Madonna Lily)

OXALIS (Ready in July)

For conservatory, greenhouse and window garden culture the Oxalis is ideal. It succeeds anywhere and with any one, flowering often in 6 to 8 weeks after planting.

		Each	Doz.	100
Grand Duchess.	Yellow.	$0.05	$0.40	$2.00
" "	White	.05	.40	2.00
" "	Pink	.05	.40	2.00
" "	Lavender	.05	.40	2.00
Bermuda Buttercup. Yellow, first size...		.05	.40	2.00
Bowel. Large flowering; rich pink......		.05	.45	2.50

MISCELLANEOUS HARDY LILIES
(Ready in Nov.)

	Each	Doz.	100
Auratum (Golden Banded Lily). White; spotted crimson, with band of yellow in centre of each petal.			
Large Bulbs, 8 to 9 inch circum........	$0.35	$3.75	$30.00
Mammoth Bulbs, 9 to 11 inch circum....	.45	4.75	35.00
Monster Bulbs, 11 to 13 inch circum....	.75	7.50	55.00
Batemanni. Apricot colored...............	.75	7.50	
Brownii. White inside, outside brown....	.75	7.50	
Canadense. Yellow, spotted black inside..	.20	2.00	15.00
Canadense Rubrum. Crimson, black spots	.30	3.00	17.00
Elegans, Leonard Joerg. Apricot pink....	.20	2.00	15.00
Hansoni. Flowers reddish orange.........	.75	7.50	50.00
Henryi. Orange yellow...................	.75	7.50	50.00
Krameri. Blush pink....................	.75	7.50	
Macranthum. Giant golden banded lily	.80	8.00	
Melpomene. Pink, spotted dark red.			
Large Bulbs, 8 to 9 inch circum.........	.35	3.75	30.00
Mammoth Bulbs, 9 to 11 inch circum....	.45	4.75	35.00
Monster Bulbs, 11 to 13 inch circum....	.75	7.50	55.00
Regale (Myriophyllum). White, shaded yellow	1.00	10.00	
Rubro-Vittatum. Spotted crimson.........	1.00	10.00	
Speciosum Album. Pure white.			
Large Bulbs, 8 to 9 inch circum.........	.35	3.75	30.00
Mammoth Bulbs, 9 to 11 inch circum....	.45	4.75	35.00
Speciosum Magnificum. Deep pink, spotted crimson.			
Large Bulbs, 8 to 9 inch circum........	.35	3.75	30.00
Mammoth Bulbs, 9 to 11 inch circum....	.45	4.75	35.00
Monster Bulbs, 11 to 13 inch circum....	.75	7.50	55.00
Speciosum Rubrum or Roseum. Delicate pink, spotted red.			
Large Bulbs, 8 to 9 inch circum.........	.35	3.75	30.00
Mammoth Bulbs, 9 to 11 inch circum...	.45	4.75	35.00
Monster Bulbs, 11 to 13 inch circum....	.75	7.50	55.00
Superbum. (Turk's Cap Lily). Orange Red	.25	2.50	15.00
Tenuifolium. (Coral Lily). Scarlet......	.20	2.00	15.00
Tigrinum Splendens (Tiger Lily). Orange, spotted black.			
Single flowering	.20	2.00	15.00
Double flowering	.35	3.50	25.00
Umbellatum. Orange scarlet.............	.20	2.50	17.50
Wittei. White, yellow band.............	1.25	12.50	

Our General Bulb Catalog is ready in September and will contain a complete list of Bulbs   (oe)

MICHELL'S "DISTINCTIVE" FLOWER SEEDS

FOR SUMMER AND EARLY FALL SOWING

For Complete List of Flower Seeds, see our General Catalogue for 1920

ACHILLEA (Milfoil or Yarrow)

	Large Pkt.	Pkt.
Ptarmica, Fl. Pl., "The Pearl." Tall erect plants; pure white double flowers; hardy perennial; 2 ft. $0.65 $0.10

ACONITUM (Monk's Hood or Helmet Flower)

Hardy perennial, thriving best in semi-shady situations; curious hood-shaped flowers in clusters; 4 feet; August-September.

	Large Pkt.	Pkt.
Napellus, Blue ... $0.30 $0.05

AGROSTEMMA (Rose of Heaven, Mullein Pink)

Coronaria. Erect growing plants with silvery foliage and crimson flowers; hardy perennial; 2½ to 3 feet; June to August ... .20 .05

ALYSSUM

	Large Pkt.	Pkt.
Lilac Queen. Dwarf and compact; flowers lilac. $0.40 $0.10
Little Dorritt. Extremely dwarf and compact, with miniature white flowers ... oz., 90c. .20 .05
Little Gem. Dwarf compact plants, densely covered with large pure white flowers; height, 4 inches ... oz., 75c. .20 .05
Saxatile Compactum (Basket of Gold). Showy golden yellow flowers; hardy perennial; 1 ft. oz., $1.25 .25 .05
Sweet. Of trailing habit, with pure white flowers; 6 inches ... oz., 40c. .20 .05

AMPELOPSIS (Boston or Japanese Ivy)

Veitchi. A hardy perennial climber with olive green leaves, which turn to scarlet in the autumn ... oz., 50c. .20 .10

ANCHUSA (Sea Bugloss)

Italica "Dropmore." A hardy perennial plant, 4 feet high, with flowers of a lovely gentian blue ... .30 .15

ANTHEMIS (Hardy Marguerite)

Tinctoria Kelwayi. A handsome hardy perennial; daisy-like bright yellow flowers; 2 feet ... .30 .10

ANTIRRHINUM (Snapdragon)

A splendid plant for beds or borders and one of our choicest cut flowers; extensively forced under glass during the winter.

MICHELL'S GIANT ANTIRRHINUMS

Spikes, 2 to 3 feet in length, with giant flowers.

	Large Pkt.	Pkt.
Michell's Giant Salmon Pink. Long spikes of flowers of a delicate salmon pink color $0.50 $0.15
Silver Pink. A fine variety; long spikes and a profuse bloomer. Original pkt., $1.00.
Giant Garnet ... .25 .10
Giant Pink ... .25 .10
Giant Scarlet ... .25 .10
Giant Striped ... .25 .10
Giant Venus. Shell pink on white ground ... .40 .15
Giant White ... .25 .10
Giant Yellow ... .25 .10
Collection, one packet each six colors, 50c.
Giant Mixed. All colors ... oz., 90c. .25 .10

ANTIRRHINUMS—Various Sorts

The Semi-Dwarf sorts grow about 18 inches high, with large flowers over most of the stem.

		Large Pkt.	Pkt.
Semi-Dwarf. Bride. Pure white $0.30 $0.10
" Cultivation. Chamois, shaded pink. .25
" Daphne. Carmine pink, white throat .25 .10
" Defiance. Fiery scarlet .25 .10
" Firebrand. Rich deep red .25 .10
" Golden Queen. Golden yellow .25 .10
" Mixed. All colors ... oz., $1.00 .25 .10
" Mont Blanc. Pure white .25 .10
" Pink Gem. Rose pink .25
" Rose Queen. Rich rose .25 .10
Tall Mixed. Regular strain ... oz., 75c. .20 .05
Tom Thumb Mixed. All colors; 12 inches .25 .10

Ask for Cultural Leaflet No. 201 on the growing of Antirrhinums.

ANEMONE (Wind Flower)

A dainty spring flower with bright cup-shaped blossoms; splendid for cutting; perennial.

	Large Pkt.	Pkt.
Coronaria Mixed. All colors; 1 foot $0.20 $0.05
St. Brigid, or Poppy. Flowers of large size; semi-double and double; 1 foot .40 .15

Aquilegia (Columbine) Long Spurred

AQUILEGIAS OR COLUMBINES

A graceful spring flowering plant; exquisitely spurred flowers on stems 2 feet above the fern-like foliage.

	Large Pkt.	Pkt.
California Hybrida. Mixed colors; long spurs $0.40 $0.10
Chrysantha. Bright golden yellow .50 .10
Coerulea. (Rocky Mountain Columbine). Large flowers, violet-blue and white .40 .10
Flabellata Nana Alba. Dwarf; white .20 .10
Haylodgensis Delicatissima. Satiny rose .50 .20
Long Spurred Hybrids. Flowers of many rich and varied colors, with long spurs .40 .10
Rose Queen. Pink, white centre .50 .15
Double Mixed. All colors ... oz., 90c. .20 .05
Single Mixed. All colors ... oz., 75c. .20 .05

ARABIS (Rock Cress)

Alpina. Early spring flowering perennial; especially adapted for edging and rockery; plants form a dense carpet completely covered with pure white blossoms; 6 inches .20 .05

ASPARAGUS

	100 Seeds	Pkt.
Hatcheri. Of dense and symmetrical growth; valuable for decorative use, also for specimen pot plants $1.00 $0.25
Plumosus Nanus. An excellent plant for house or conservatory decoration 1.00 .25
Sprengeri. One of the best plants to grow in hanging baskets for greenhouse in winter or for outdoors in the summer .50 .10

(oe)

ASPERULA (Woodruff)

Large Pkt. Pkt.

Odorata. Dwarf spring flowers of purest white; thrives in shady situations; perennial; 1 foot; May $0.30 $0.05

ASTER, PERENNIAL (Michaelmas Daisy)

Large Pkt. Pkt.

Choice Mixed. A showy perennial plant; star-like single flowers; 2 to 3 feet.................... $0.30 : $0.10

AURICULA (Primula Auricula)

Choice Mixed. These early flowering perennial plants resemble primroses and have multi-colored flowers in great variety; 6 inches............... .65   .10

BAPTISIA (False Indigo)

Australis. A strong-growing perennial plant about 2 feet high, with dark green, deeply cut foliage and spikes of dark blue flowers in June and July .25   .05

BOCCONIA (Plume Poppy)

Cordata. A splendid hardy perennial, with glaucous green foliage and spikes 2 to 3 feet long of creamy white flowers; 5 feet.................. .20   .05

BOLTONIA (False Chamomile)

Latisquama. A showy hardy perennial, with daisy-like flowers; color, pink, tinged with lilac; 4 to 6 feet; July to September................... .30   .10

BROWALLIA

Elegant free flowering plants; blooms finely in the winter if the plants are lifted and cut back; 18 inches.

Large Pkt. Pkt.

Elata Coerulea. Sky-blue flowers............. $0.25 $0.05
Speciosa Major. Large ultramarine blue flowers; desirable as a pot plant for winter and spring flowering .... .50   .10

CALCEOLARIA

Our strains of Calceolaria have a wide reputation as to large size and rich and varied colors of the flowers.

Large Pkt. Pkt.

Hybrida Grandiflora, Tall Mixed. Large flowering, rich, self-colored flowers saved from a choice collection; 18 inches...................... $0.75 $0.25
Hybrid Grandiflora, Pumila Compacta. Of dwarf, compact growth; trusses of large, self-colored and spotted flowers; 1 foot................. .75   .25
Sutton's Perfection. Choicest mixed. Original packet 1.25

CALLIOPSIS (Coreopsis)

California Sunbeams. Large flowers beautifully formed; various shades of yellow and brown.... .20   .10
Lanceolata Grandiflora. Single golden yellow flowers of graceful form; invaluable for cutting; flowers uninterruptedly the entire summer ....oz., 60c. .20   .10

CANDYTUFT (Iberis)

Sempervirens. Dwarf spring flowering perennial; flowers glistening white; May; 1 foot.......... .50   .10

CARNATION

Desirable for greenhouse culture in winter as well as for the garden in summer.

Large Pkt. Pkt.

Chabaud's Everblooming Mixed. Blooms in five months after being sown.................... $0.50 $0.15
Choice Mixed. Double border.................. .50   .10
Early Vienna. Large double flowers in choicest mixture; 1 foot............................ .40   .10

MARGUERITE CARNATIONS

Excelsior Mixed. Immense flowers in all the beautiful shades .... .40   .15
Pink .... .40   .10
Scarlet .... .40   .10
White .... .40   .10
Yellow .... .40   .10
Choice Mixed ....oz., $1.50 .25   .10
Ask for Cultural Leaflet No. 213 on the growing of Carnations from seed.

Campanula—Media

CAMPANULA MEDIA (Canterbury Bell)

Showy, hardy biennial growing about 3 feet high, with large bell-shaped flowers. Sow from June 1st till September 1st; after frost has set in protect with leaves and straw.

	Oz.	Large Pkt.	Pkt.
Single Blue	$0.75	$0.20	$0.05
" Pink	.75	.20	.05
" White	.75	.20	.05
" Mixed	.60	.20	.05
Double Mixed	¼ oz., 50c.	.30	.05

CAMPANULA CALYCANTHEMA

(Cup and Saucer)

These produce beautiful, large single flowers, resembling a cup and saucer; they require the same treatment as above.

	Large Pkt.	Pkt.
Blue	$0.40	$0.10
Pink	.40	.10
White	.40	.10
Mixed	¼ oz., 60c. .30	.10

CAMPANULAS OR BELLFLOWERS

PERENNIAL VARIETIES

These are among our best known hardy perennials; the tall varieties are fine for cutting while the dwarf sorts make excellent border plants; all have dainty bell-shaped flowers.

	Large Pkt.	Pkt.
Carpatica (Carpathian Hare Bell). Blue compact tufts not exceeding 8 inches; flowers clear blue, held erect; blooms in June and July	$0.25	$0.05
Carpatica, Alba. Pure white	.25	.05
Persicifolia Grandiflora (Peach Bells). Blue; spikes 4 feet tall with bell-shaped flowers	.40	.15
Persicifolia Grandiflora, Alba. Pure white	.40	.15
Pyramidalis (Chimney Bell Flower). Perfect pyramids 6 feet high crowded with large bell-shaped flowers, blue and white mixed	.30	.05

CENTAUREA (Perennial)

Large feathery flowers; splendid for cutting; blooms from July to September.

Large Pkt. Pkt.

Montana. Blue; 1 foot...................... $0.30 $0.10

CERASTIUM (Snow in Summer)

Tomentosum. Dwarf, white-leaved edging plant; flowers white; perennial; 4 inches........... .40   .15

CHRYSANTHEMUM (Perennial)

Japanese Hybrids. Large flowers of the finest types; an extra choice mixture; seed sown in spring will produce flowering plants by fall; 2 feet .... .65   .15
King Edward VII. Flowers extra large; pure white and of perfect form.................. .25   .10
Shasta Daisy, "Alaska." The finest of all; single white flowers on long stems; 2 feet.......... .50   .20

(oe)

CINERARIA

Our Grandiflora Prize Strain is the best procurable, producing immense trusses of the largest flowers, often measuring up to 4 inches across.

	Large Pkt.	Pkt.
Grandiflora Prize Dwarf. Mixed colors	$0.75	$0.35
Grandiflora Prize Medium Tall. Mixed colors	.75	.35
Hybrida. Choice mixed colors	.65	.25
Matador. Large, bright red flowers	.75	.35
Stellata (Sutton's). Medium sized star-like flowers. Original pkt		1.00
Stellata Hybrida. Mixed colors	.75	.25

Ask for Cultural Leaflet No. 203 on the growing of Cinerarias.

CLEMATIS

Perennial climbers; fine for arbors, verandas, etc.

	Large Pkt.	Pkt.
Flammula. Feathery white, fragrant flowers	$0.20	$0.05
Paniculata. (Japanese Virgin's Bower). The beautiful autumn-flowering variety, admired for its fragrant white, star-shaped flowers	.20	.10

CYCLAMEN

Most beautiful winter and spring flowering plants for the window and greenhouse. Not only are the flowers of striking beauty, but the foliage is also highly ornamental.

MICHELL'S GIANT SHOW

Grown for us by a specialist who has received numerous first prizes for the large size and beautiful coloring of the flowers.

	100 Seeds	Pkt.
Bright Red	$2.50	$0.50
Dark Blood Red	2.50	.50
Glory of Wandsbek. Salmon red	2.50	.50
Perle of Zehlendorf. Salmon pink	2.50	.50
Pure White	2.50	.50
Rose of Marienthal. Bright pink	2.50	.50
White with Carmine Eye	2.50	.50
Mixed. All colors	2.00	.40

MICHELL'S LARGE FLOWERING

	100 Seeds	Pkt.
Duke of Connaught. Crimson	$2.00	$0.50
Excelsior. White with red eye	2.00	.50
Grandiflora Alba. White	2.00	.50
Princess of Wales. Pink	2.00	.50
Salmon Queen. Salmon pink	2.00	.50
St. George. Flowers a beautiful salmon color; leaves margined with silver	2.00	.50
Mixed. All colors	1.75	.40

VARIOUS CYCLAMEN

Mrs. Buckston. Frilled and waved flowers; color delicate salmon. Original pkt		.75
Papilio (Butterfly). The edges of the flowers are beautifully fringed, or waved; mixed colors	1.75	.40

Ask for Cultural Leaflet No. 215 on the growing of Cyclamen.

DAISY, ENGLISH DOUBLE (Bellis Perennis)

These are favorite perennials; seed should be sown from June 1st till September, transplanted in the fall and they will flower the following spring; 4 inches.

	Large Pkt.	Pkt.
Longfellow. Large double pink flowers	$0.50	$0.10
Monstrosa, Pink. These surpass all strains of this popular plant in strong growth, and in the abundance of extra large, perfectly double flowers	.65	.25
Monstrosa, White	.65	.25
Monstrosa, Mixed	.65	.25
Snowball. Purest white; large and double	.50	.10
Double Mixed. Finest quality	.40	.10

DIANTHUS (Hardy Garden Pinks)

Clove Scented. Double and semi-double varieties, in-beautiful colors; fragrant		.40	.10
Double Scotch. Choice mixed colors		.40	.15
Erfurt. Of dwarf, compact growth; blooms early; mixed colors		.50	.10
Latifolius Atrococcineus Fl. Pl. (Everblooming Hybrid Sweet William). Double scarlet		.50	.10
Pheasant's Eye. Single white fringed flowers with dark centre	oz., 75c.	.20	.05

DICTAMNUS (Gas Plant)

Fraxinella. Showy bushy plants 2½ feet high, purple red flowers; perennial; June and July	.20	.05

DELPHINIUM

(Hardy Larkspur)

Delphinium—Kelway's Giant

One of the finest hardy perennials; easily grown from seed; effective in beds, masses or borders.

Belladonna. One of the most continuous blooming varieties; large spikes of clear turquoise blue; 5 feet. Pkt., 25c.; 65c. per large pkt.

Chinese Grandiflorum. A dwarf strain with loose branches and sprays of bright blue flowers; 2 feet. Pkt., 25c. per large pkt.; oz., 90c.

Chinese Grandiflorum Album. Pure white flowers. Pkt., 5c.; 25c. per large pkt.; oz., 90c.

Elatum (Bee Larkspur). Rich blue; 4 feet. Pkt., 10c.; 30c. per large pkt.; oz., $1.75.

Formosum. Deep blue; 3 feet. Pkt., 10c.; 30c. per large pkt.; oz., $1.50.

Formosum Coelestinum. Sky blue. Pkt., 15c.; 50c. per large pkt.

Kelway's Giant. Plants are of strong, vigorous growth, with immense spikes of large flowers; many shades of blue; 5 to 7 feet. Pkt., 15c.; 50c. per large pkt.

Rev. E. Lascelles. Large double, deep blue flowers with white centre. Pkt., 15c.; 65c. per large pkt.

Zalil. Sulphur yellow; 4 feet. Pkt., 10c.; large pkt., 50c.

Hybridum Mixed. Very choice; 4 feet. Pkt., 5c.; 20c. per large pkt.; oz., 75c.

DIGITALIS (Foxglove)

Ornamental hardy plants; long spikes of beautiful tubular-shaped flowers; blooms during June and July; 4 to 5 feet.

	Oz.	Large Pkt.	Pkt.
Gloxiniaeflora, Pink	$1.25	$0.25	$0.10
" Purple	1.25	.25	.10
" White	1.25	.25	.10
" Mixed	.90	.20	.05
Grandiflora. Yellow	.90	.20	.05
Monstrosa (Mammoth Foxglove). The tall spikes are surmounted by one monstrous flower; all colors mixed	1.50	.30	.10

EUPATORIUM

Fraseri. Tall bushy plants with loose heads of feathery white flowers; perennial; 2 feet	.20	.10

FERNS

Very desirable plants for ferneries.

Adiantum (Maiden Hair). Mixed	.65	.15
Pteris Varieties. Mixed	.65	.15
All Sorts Mixed. Choice collection	.65	.15

We can also furnish all other good varieties of fern spores.

GAILLARDIA (Blanket Flower)

One of the most showy of hardy perennials; spikes of gorgeously colored flowers of immense size.

		Large Pkt.	Pkt.
Grandiflora Compacta. A compact variety; mixed colors; 12 to 15 inches	oz., 90c.	$0.20	$0.10
Grandiflora Sanguinea. Blood red flowers; 2 ft		.25	.15
Grandiflora Semi-Double. Mixed		.25	.10
Grandiflora Superba. Splendid mixed, 2 feet,	oz., 90c.	.90	.10

(oe)

GERBERA (Transvaal Daisy)

Splendid greenhouse perennials with large fine-leaved, daisy-like flowers; splendid for pot plants or cutting. 100 Seeds Pkt.
Jamesoni Gigantea. Large flowers of bright scarlet.$1.25 . $0.25
Jamesoni Hybrida. These hybrids include a wonderful range of brilliant colors and shades...... 1.00   .25

GEUM

Large Pkt. Pkt.
Atrosanguineum Fl. Pl. Hardy perennial with large, showy, double, dark crimson flowers; 1½ feet 25   .10

GYPSOPHILA (Baby's Breath)

Paniculata. Hardy perennial; flowers in graceful sprays of white; 2 feet......oz., 90c.. .20 .05
Paniculata, Fl. Pl. Double white................20

HELENIUM (Sneeze-Wort)

Autumnale Superbum. Perennial; large heads of golden yellow flowers; 5 to 6 feet...........30   .10

Hollyhock—Chater's Double

HOLLYHOCK

A popular and desirable hardy perennial plant; excellent for planting among shrubbery or forming a background for other flowers; 6 to 7 feet.
Oz. Large Pkt. Pkt.
Allegheny. Semi-double; mammoth flowers, edges fringed and laciniated; mixed$1.00 $0.25 $0.10
Chater's Double, Maroon .... 1.25   .25   .10
"   "   Pink .... 1.25   .25   .10
"   "   Red .... 1.25   .25   .10
"   "   Salmon .... 1.25   .25   .10
"   "   White .... 1.25   .25   .10
"   "   Yellow .... 1.25   .25   .10
"   "   Mixed .... 1.00   .25   .10
Collection, one packet each of above 6 colors............   .50
Double Ever-blooming Mixed. Colors range from white to deep black, yellow, pink, red and purple.........................1.25   .30   .15
Single Ever-blooming Mixed.............1.00   .25   .10
Single Mixed 90   .20   .10

HELIOPSIS (Orange Sunflower)

Large Pkt. Pkt.
Pitcheriana. A handsome hardy perennial; deep orange yellow flowers; excellent for cutting......$0.20 $0.10

HEUCHERA (Alum Root)

Sanguinea. Splendid plant; spikes of vivid crimson flowers; excellent for cutting; 1 foot 50   .10

HIBISCUS (Marshmallow)

Showy plants for mixed beds or shrubbery borders; large, beautiful bell-shaped flowers; perennial.   Large Pkt. Pkt.
Crimson Eye. Large white flowers with crimson centre; 4 feet........................$0.20 $0.10
Golden Bowl. Giant yellow, maroon centre...... .20   .10
Moscheutos. Rosy red with dark centre........ .20   .05
New Giant (Mallow Marvel). Mixed............ .25   .15

IRIS (Flowering Flag)

Kaempferi (Japanese Iris). Perennial; blooms the second year from seed; mixed colors...........   .20   .10

LATHYRUS LATIFOLIUS
(Everlasting or Perennial Pea)

Free flowering, hardy perennial climber with clusters of flowers resembling Sweet Peas; excellent for cutting.
Oz. Large Pkt. Pkt.
Crimson. Brilliant $0.75 $0.20 $0.10
Pink Beauty. Bright rosy-pink......... 1.00   .25   .10
White .... .90   .20   .10
Choice Mixed. All colors............ .75   .20   .05

LAVENDER

Well-known perennial plant, bearing long spikes of fragrant blue flowers; 18 inches............   .25   .05

LOBELIA

Cardinalis (Cardinal Flower). Hardy perennial; tall spikes of bright scarlet flowers, very showy .50   .10

LUPINUS (Lupins)
Annual Varieties

Seeds sown in greenhouse during the late summer and fall months will produce an abundance of bloom for winter.
Oz. Large Pkt. Pkt.
Rich Blue $0.50 $0.20 $0.05
Pink .... .50   .20   .05
Scarlet, White Tipped............... .50   .20   .05
Sky Blue .... .50   .20   .05
White .... .50   .20   .05
Mixed. Annual varieties............ .40   .20   .05

LUPINUS (Perennial Varieties)

Polyphyllus, Blue .... .20   .05
"   Roseus. Pink .... .25   .10
"   Somerset. Yellow .... .40   .15
"   White .... .20   .05
"   Mixed ....oz., 40c. .20   .05
Ask for Cultural Leaflet No. 217 on the culture of Lupinus.

LYCHNIS

Perennials of easy culture; excellent for massing in large beds or borders.   Large Pkt. Pkt.
Chalcedonica (Rose Campion). Fine scarlet cross-like flowers; 2 feet; July......oz., 60c. $0.20 $0.05
Haageana. Brilliant, large, orange, scarlet, pink, or crimson flowers, mixed; 1 foot; July.........   .50   .10

MIGNONETTE

Seed may be sown at intervals during the summer for a succession of bloom; may also be forced in greenhouses during the winter.   Large Pkt. Pkt.
Allen's Defiance. Spikes invariably attain a height of 12 to 15 inches; deliciously fragrant..oz., 60c.$0.20 $0.10
Bismarck. Compact plant of strong growth; stout spikes of large flowers................oz., 90c. .15   .10
Golden Machet. Large golden yellow.....oz., 50c. .20   .10
Goliath. Giant spikes of red flowers......oz., 75c. .20   .10
Machet. Large reddish tinted, sweet scented flowers ....oz., 50c. .20   .10
Michell's Colossal. Flower-spikes often average 18 inches; extremely fragrant...........   .50   .15
Suteon's Giant. Reddish buff. Original pkts....   .40
Sweet Scented. The popular garden sort..oz., 30c. .15   .05
Ask for Cultural Leaflet No. 204 on the growing of Mignonette.

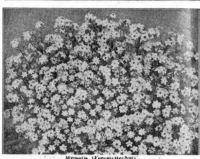

Myosotis (Forget-Me-Not)

MYOSOTIS (Forget-Me-Not)

Neat little plants with star-shaped flowers; for spring flowering sow in July or August.

	Large Pkt.	Pkt.
Alpestris Victoria. Of bushy habit; bearing large bright blue flowers; very fine; 6 inches........$0.30		$0.10
Dissitiflora. Attractive deep blue flowers.........50		.10
Eliza Fanrobert. Large flowering; bright blue....30		.10
Grandiflora Alba. Large white flowers; 8 inches.30		.10
Grandiflora Rosa. Large pink flowers; 8 inches..30		.10
Palustris. The true Forget-Me-Not; bright blue flowers; 8 inches...........................50		.10
Palustris Semperflorens. Dwarf; blooms the entire season; deep blue...........................50		.10
Royal Blue. Upright grower; blue; 1 foot.........40		.10
Ruth Fischer. Plant of neat, compact habit; flowers large and of a lovely sky blue..../..........65		.25
Choice Mixed. Blue, rose and white......oz., $1.00 .20		.05

MICHELL'S GIANT PANSIES

Seed sown in frames during July and August and transplanted later gives us the main crop of flowers the following spring.

PANSIES IN MIXTURES

	Large Pkt.	Pkt.
Michell's Giant Exhibition. A blending of our own containing only the very choicest secured from the leading Pansy specialists; flowers of immense size, very heavy texture and of the most brilliant colors. Per oz., $10.00; $3.00 per ¼ oz.; per ⅛ oz., $1.75 ....$0.65		$0.25
Bugnot, Odier and Cassier. A superb mixture of giant blotched varieties. ....⅛ oz., $1.00 .65		.25
Giant Trimardeau. Very large flowering; all colors mixed....¼ oz., $1.00 .40		.10
Mad. Perret. Early flowering, fragrant, especially rich in red shades. ....¼ oz., $1.25 .65		.25
Masterpiece (Frilled Pansy). Flowers beautifully curled or waved........ ....⅛ oz., $1.00 .65		.25
Odier or Blotched. Beautiful strain. ....¼ oz., $1.25 .65		.15
Parisian Large Stained. Choice colors. ....¼ oz., $1.25 .65		.15
Triumph of the Giants, Mixed. Immense flowers of great brilliancy and richness of coloring, including many new and rare shades. Per oz., $11.00; $3.25 per ¼ oz.; per ⅛ oz., $2.00 75		.50
Finest English Mixed.........oz., $2.25 .30		.10
Very Fine Mixed.............oz., $1.50 .25		.05

Ask for Cultural Leaflet No. 209 on the growing of Pansies.

GIANT PANSIES—Separate Colors

	¼ Oz.	Large Pkt.	Pkt.
Giant Prize, Azure Blue. Violet blue....$1.25		$0.50	$0.15
" " Black Blue. Dark velvety.... 1.25		.50	.15
" " Emperor William. Ultramarine blue 1.25		.50	.15
" " Hortensia Red. Scarlet..... 1.25		.50	.15
" " King of the Blacks. Black.. 1.25		.50	.15
" " Lord Beaconsfield. Violet... 1.25		.50	.15
" " Peacock. Upper petals blue, lower petals deep claret; white margin 1.50		.50	.15
" " Snow Queen. Pure white.... 1.25		.50	.15
" " Striped and Mottled........ 1.25		.50	.15
" " White with dark eye........ 1.25		.50	.15
" " Pure Yellow 1.25		.50	.15
" " Yellow with dark eye....... 1.25		.50	.15

SPECIAL OFFER: We will send 6 packets of any of the above varieties of Giant Pansies for 75c; or the entire 12 pkts. for $1.40.

PANSIES—Regular Sorts in Separate Colors

	Oz.	Large Pkt.	Pkt.
Belgian Striped. Showy.................$2.75		$0.30	$0.10
Emperor William. Ultramarine blue..... 2.75		.30	.10
Faust (King of the Blacks). Almost black 2.75		.30	.10
Gold Margined. Purple, golden edge...... 2.75		.30	.10
Havana Brown 2.75		.30	.10
Lord Beaconsfield. Violet............. 2.75		.30	.10
Mahogany Colored 2.75		.30	.10
Silver Edged. Purple, silver edge....... 2.75		.30	.10
Snow Queen. Pure white............. 2.75		.30	.10
White with dark eye.................. 2.75		.30	.10
Yellow Gem. Pure yellow.............. 2.75		.30	.10
Yellow with dark eye................. 2.75		.30	.10

SPECIAL OFFER: We will send 6 packages of any of the above varieties of regular sorts of Pansies for 50c; or the entire 12 packets for 90c.

Michell's Giant Exhibition Pansy

PENTSTEMON (Beard Tongue)

A perennial plant producing large spikes of flowers.

	Large Pkt.	Pkt.
Sensation. Large spikes of gloxinia-like flowers of brilliant colors; 2 feet; requires protection.	$0.40	$0.15
Mixed. Choice colors; 3 feet,	.20	.05

HARDY PHLOX

Decussata. Plants 2 to 3 feet high; flowers in all bright colors; sow seeds late in fall and they will germinate in the spring .... .40 .10

PHYSOSTEGIA (False Dragon Head)

A pretty hardy perennial, bearing freely, delicate tubular flowers; 3 to 4 feet; July-August.

	Large Pkt.	Pkt.
Virginica. Pink	$0.25	$0.10
Alba. White	.30	.10

PLATYCODON (Chinese Bell Flower)

One of the best hardy perennials; large bell-shaped flowers; excellent for borders or among shrubbery; 2 to 3 feet.

	Large Pkt	Pkt
Grandiflorum, Blue	$0.30	$0.05
Grandiflorum, White	.30	.05
Japonicus Fl. Pl. (Double Japanese Bell Flower). Large, glossy, deep blue flowers	.50	.15

POLYANTHUS (Primula Elatior)

Gold Laced. Flowers of brilliant colors, with distinct yellow edge	.50	.15
Double Mixed. Beautiful colors	.65	.15
English Mixed. All colors	.30	.10

Oriental Poppy

POPPY (Perennial)

This class of Poppies is unequalled for general effectiveness and brilliancy of display.

	Large Pkt	Pkt.
Giant Scarlet (Bracteatum). Large flowers; 3 feet.	$0.20	$0.10
Iceland (Nudicaule). White, 1 foot	.30	.10
" Yellow	.30	.10
" Double Mixed	.30	.10
" Single Mixed. A wide range of colors	.20	.10
Orientale. Extra large flowers; deep scarlet	.20	.10
" Beauty of Livermore. Crimson with black blotch	.50	.10
" Mrs. Perry. Rich salmon pink	.50	.10
" Hybrids. Beautiful flowers of large size, mixed colors ..... ¼ oz., 50¢.	.30	.10

PRIMULA

FRINGED CHINESE PRIMROSE

These are among our finest winter and spring blooming pot plants for decorations in the home or conservatory. Our seed has been grown for us by a Primula Specialist, and cannot be excelled for size and brilliancy of colors. Our strains have won many first prizes.

	Large Pkt.	Pkt.
Alba Magnifica. Large pure white flowers.	$0.75	$0.40
Chiswick Red. Brilliant red	.75	.40
Duchess. Large; white with zone of rosy carmine, yellow eye	.75	.40
Holborn Blue. A beautiful shade	.75	.40
Kermesina Splendens. Crimson	.75	.50
Pink Pearl (New). Brilliant pink		.50
Rosy Morn. Delicate pink	.75	.40
Stellata (Sutton's). Excellent pot plant; mixed		1.00
Michell's Prize Mixture. This mixture contains only the finest sorts selected from the best strains	.75	.25
Imported Collection. 8 varieties		.75

PRIMULA OBCONICA GIGANTEA

A great improvement over the old type; flowers much larger, and produced in greater abundance.

	Large Pkt.	Pkt.
Lilacina. Pale lilac	$0.65	$0.20
Rosea. Pink	.65	.20
Kermesina. Crimson	.65	.20
Alba. White	.65	.20
Hybrida Mixed	.65	.20

PRIMULA OBCONICA GRANDIFLORA

Fimbriata. Flowers fringed; mixed colors	.65	.15
Vésuvius. Deep crimson	.65	.25

PRIMULA—VARIOUS SORTS

Kewensis (Verbena Scented Yellow Primrose). Spikes each 12 to 18 inches long; color, soft yellow; very fragrant	.65	.25
Malacoides. Resembles Primula Forbesi, but the flowers are much larger; if grown in a greenhouse it will bloom in four to five months after sowing and continue for a long time; color, a pretty light lilac	.65	.20
Malacoides Alba. Flowers pure white	.65	.20
Malacoides Alba Plena. A new variety with double white flowers		.75
Malacoides Superba. Deep rosy pink		.25

HARDY PRIMROSES

Excellent early spring blooming plants; hardy, though in very cold localities they should have slight protection.

	Large Pkt.	Pkt.
Veris (English Cowslip). Fragrant; flowers of various colors; 6 inches; mixed	$0.30	$0.10
Vulgaris (English Primrose). The common hardy English variety; canary yellow	.30	.10

Ask for Cultural Leaflet No. 206 on the growing of Primulas.

PUERARIA THUNBERGIANA
(Kudzu Vine)

One of the fastest growing hardy climbing plants; grows 8 to 10 feet the first year from seed; after the first year it will grow 30 to 50 feet in a season; rosy purple pea-shaped blossoms toward the end of August .... .20 .10

PYRETHRUM (Perennial)

Handsome hardy perennial plants for the herbaceous border; flowers showy and excellent for cutting.

	Large Pkt.	Pkt.
Roseum. Flowers bright rose color; July; 2 feet	$0.50	$0.10
Uliginosum. Large, single white flowers; September; 3 to 4 ft.	.50	.10
Hybridum Single Mixed. Large flowers ranging in color from light pink to deep red, with bright yellow centres; July; 2 feet	.40	.10
Hybridum Double Mixed	.65	.25

RUDBECKIA (Coneflower)

	Large Pkt.	Pkt.
Newmani. Large yellow flowers with black centre; perennial; 3 feet; all summer.	$0.40	$0.10
Purpurea (Giant Purple Coneflower). Hardy perennial; reddish purple flowers, with dark brown disc; 3 feet.	.30	.10

SALVIA

	Large Pkt.	Pkt.
Farinacea. A perennial variety, but best treated as an annual; color, light blue; 2 feet.	.30	.10

SCABIOSA

Handsome perennial border plants, flowering the entire season; 3 feet.

	Large Pkt.	Pkt.
Caucasica. Soft blue.	$0.50	$0.10
Caucasica Alba. Pure white.	.50	.10
Japonica. Lavender blue.	.20	.10

SCHIZANTHUS (Butterfly Flower)

One of our finest annuals, bearing a profusion of pretty butterfly-like flowers of various colors; desirable for winter and spring blooming in pots.

	Large Pkt.	Pkt.
Grandiflorus Maximus. Flowers extra large, and of various colors.		$0.25
Hybridus Grandiflorus. Compact plants, with flowers of many shades and of orchid-like appearance; 12 inches.	$0.20	.10
Pink Beauty. A beautiful shade of rose pink.		.50
Wisetonensis. A showy variety, largely used as a pot plant for the house or conservatory; flowers range from white with yellow centre to pink with brown centre.	.40	.20
Mixed. Various colors.	.20	.05

SMILAX

A desirable greenhouse climber of great value for floral decorations; seed should be soaked 24 hours in warm water before sowing.....oz., 50c. 20 .... .10

STATICE (Everlasting Flower)

Latifolia. Splendid hardy perennial, either for the border or rockery; panicles of small blue flowers, which can be dried and used for winter bouquets; 1 foot .... .30 .10

Single Sweet William

Michell's "Distinctive" Stocks

The seeds we offer are hand-saved from pot-grown specimens and will produce a large percentage of double flowers.

MICHELL'S "NICE" STOCK

An early flowering strain; remarkable free bloomer; large double, fragrant flowers; fine for cutting. For winter blooming, sow from July to September.

	Large Pkt.	Pkt.
Abundance. Dwarf spreading habit; color, carmine rose	$0.40	$0.15
Beauty of Nice. Delicate soft pink.	.40	.15
Crimson King. Brilliant fiery crimson.	.40	.15
La Brilliante. Rich brilliant crimson.	.40	.15
Midsummer Night. Deep dark violet.	.40	.15
Mont Blanc. Pure white.	.40	.15
Queen Alexandra. Delicate lavender.	.40	.15
Choice Mixed. All colors.	.40	.15

MICHELL'S FLOWER MARKET STOCK

This is the ideal stock for either gardens, cutting or forcing under glass. Plants branch freely and produce from 10 to 15 heavy spikes of extra large perfect flowers; height, 2 feet.

	Large Pkt.	Pkt.		Large Pkt.	Pkt.
Blood Red	$0.40	$0.15	Rose Pink	$0.40	$0.15
Dark Blue	.40	.15	White	.40	.15
Flesh Pink	.40	.15	Mixed	.40	.15
Light Blue	.40	.15			

LARGE FLOWERED DWARF TEN-WEEK STOCK

	Large Pkt.	Pkt.		Large Pkt.	Pkt.
Blood Red	$0.30	$0.10	White	$0.30	$0.10
Light Blue	.30	.10	Yellow	.30	.10
Pink	.30	.10	Mixed	.30	.10
Purple	.30	.10			

VARIOUS STOCKS

	Large Pkt.	Pkt.
Brompton or Winter. Fine for forcing under glass or early summer flowering outdoor.	.40	.10
Princess Alice (Cut-and-Come-Again). Branching plants with double pure white flowers.	.40	.10

Ask for Cultural Leaflet No. 211 on the growing of Stocks.

STOKESIA (Cornflower or Stokes' Aster)

A very desirable hardy perennial plant, bearing freely from July to October handsome Centaurea-like blossoms, each measuring from 4 to 5 inches across; excellent for cutting; 1½ to 2 feet.

	Large Pkt.	Pkt.
Cyanea. Light blue	$0.30	$0.10
" Alba. Pure white	.30	.10

SUNFLOWER (Helianthus)

Showy perennials blooming all summer.

	Large Pkt.	Pkt.
Golden Bouquet. Single yellow flowers; 5 feet.	.30	.10
Choice Mixed. Single flowering.	.40	.10

Sweet Peas. See Next Page

SWEET ROCKET (Hesperis)

Mixed. Fragrant white and purple flowers; a desirable hardy perennial; 2 to 3 feet............ .20 .05

SWEET WILLIAM (Dianthus Barbatus)

One of the finest hardy garden plants; of easy culture, and lasting for years. The plants grow about 1½ feet high, and form fine clumps.

		Large Pkt.	Pkt.
Auricula Flowered. A beautiful class of "eyed" single varieties; all colors mixed.	oz., 90c	$0.20	$0.05
Single, Crimson	oz., 90c	.20	.05
" Pink Beauty. Salmon pink		.40	.15
" Scarlet Beauty. Deep scarlet		.40	.15
" Velvety Maroon	oz., 75c	.20	.05
" White	oz., 75c	.20	.05
" Mixed. All colors	oz., 60c	.20	.05
Double Mixed	oz., $1.00	.20	.10

Early or Winter Flowering Spencer Sweet Peas

	Pkt.	Oz.
Asta Ohn. Rich lavender	$0.15	$1.25
Blue Bird. A charming shade of blue	.15	1.25
Cherry Ripe. Cherry or salmon cerise	.15	1.25
Daybreak. Rose pink on cream ground	.15	1.25
Enchantress. Bright rose pink	.15	1.25
Fire King. Deep orange-scarlet	.15	1.25
Heatherbell. Mauve lavender	.15	1.25
Helen Lewis. Orange pink	.15	1.25
Hercules. Soft rose pink	.15	1.25
Illumination. Glowing salmon cerise	.15	1.25
Lavender King. Rich, deep lavender	.15	1.25
Lavender Nora	.15	.50
Lavender Pink	.15	1.25
Liberty. Deep sunproof crimson	.15	1.25
Mauve Beauty. Rosy mauve	.15	1.25
Meadow Lark. Rich cream	.15	1.25
Melody. Rose pink on white ground	.15	1.25
Morning Star. Deep orange scarlet in standard; with rich, orange-pink wings	.15	1.25
Mrs. A. A. Skaach. Clear, light pink	.15	1.25
Mrs. M. Spanolin. Pure white	.15	1.25
Mrs. William Sim. Salmon pink	.15	1.25
Pink Beauty. Rose pink on white ground	.15	1.25
Pink and White	.15	1.25
Primrose Beauty. Deep primrose, flushed rose	.15	1.25
Red Orchid	.15	1.25
Rose Queen. Flowers are borne freely on long stems, are of large size, and usually four flowers are produced on a stem. Color a most attractive shade of pink ¼ oz., $1.50	.50	4.00
Sankey. Large white; black seeded	.15	1.25
Snow Flake. Large pure white	.15	1.25
Snowstorm. White; large	.15	1.25
Song Bird. Pale pink on white ground	.15	1.25
Songster. Rich lavender	.15	1.25
Spring Maid. Light pink on white ground	.15	1.25
Venus. White, blushed pink	.15	1.25
Warbler. Rich mauve purple	.15	1.25
White Orchid	.15	1.25
Yarrawa. Flowers exquisitely waved, and of large size, many of them being duplex or double. Color, a pleasing shade of bright rose pink with lighter wings	.15	1.25
Zephyr. Pale blue or lavender	.15	1.25
Mixed Colors	.10	.75

WINTER FLOWERING GRANDIFLORA SWEET PEAS

	Pkt.	Oz.	¼ Lb.
Christmas Meteor. Scarlet	$0.10	$0.20	$0.60
" Pink. Pink and white	.10	.20	.60
" White (Florence Denzer)	.10	.20	.60
Earliest of All. Pink and white	.10	.20	.60
Le Marquis. Large dark blue	.10	.20	.60
Michell's Snowdrift. Pure white; black seeded; extra early	.10	.20	.60
Mrs. F. J. Delansky. Daybreak pink	.10	.20	.60
Mixed. Winter flowering	.10	.20	.60

Viola Cornuta

VIOLA CORNUTA (Tufted Pansies)

These resemble pansies in shape and form, with the additional quality that they have long stems, and bloom from early spring till late in fall.

	Large Pkt.	Pkt.
Admiration. Dark blue	$0.50	$0.10
Mauve Queen. Lovely mauve color	.50	.10
Perfection. Light blue	.50	.10
White Perfection. Pure white	.50	.10
Mixed. All colors	.40	.10

VIOLA (Scotch Bedding Pansies)

These are very free flowering and cannot be surpassed for bedding purposes; produce larger flowers than the above.

	Large Pkt.	Pkt.
Golden Gem. Yellow	$0.50	$0.15
Lutea Splendens. Rich golden yellow	.40	.10
Snowflake. Pure white	.50	.15
Mixed. From the best named Scotch varieties	.65	.25

WALLFLOWER

While these are perennials, they are not perfectly hardy; the plants should be lifted late in the fall and planted in a cold-frame, and removed to the garden again in the spring; the flowers are fragrant and splendid for cutting.

	Large Pkt.	Pkt.
Double Brown	$0.50	$0.10
" Yellow	.50	.10
" Mixed. All colors	.50	.10
Single Mixed oz., 40c.	.20	.05
Imported Collection. 6 double varieties		.50
Imported Collection. 6 single varieties		.40

Paris Extra Early. A single-flowering variety, which may be treated as an annual, flowering the first year from seed.

	Large Pkt.	Pkt.
Paris Extra Early. Blood Red	$0.20	$0.10
" " " Yellow	.20	.10
" " " Mixed. All colors oz., 60c.	.20	.10

MICHELL'S COLLECTION OF HARDY PERENNIAL FLOWER SEEDS

18 Varieties. Special Price, $1.25.
One packet each of the following:

Alyssum. Saxatile.	Hollyhock. Chater's Double.
Aquilegia. Single Mixed.	Lobelia. Cardinalis.
Calliopsis. Lanceolata.	Poppy. Orientale.
Campanula. Pyramidalis.	Pyrethrum. Single, Mixed.
Delphinium. Formosum.	Rudbeckia. Purpurea.
Dianthus. Clove Scented.	Scabiosa. Caucasica.
Digitalis. Gloxiniaeflora.	Stokesia. Cyanea.
Gaillardia. Grandiflora.	Sweet William. Double.
Gypsophila. Paniculata.	Mixture of Perennial Flowers.

MICHELL'S PERENNIAL FLOWER GARDEN MIXTURE

To create an old-fashioned wild garden or to naturalize along roads or woods we highly recommend this mixture, as it contains many hundred varieties of the choicest old-fashioned flowers. Pkt., 10c.; 40c. per oz.; per ¼ lb., $1.25.

Ask for Cultural Leaflet No. 212 on the growing of Hardy Perennials from seed.

For complete list see our General Seed Catalogue, mailed free on request

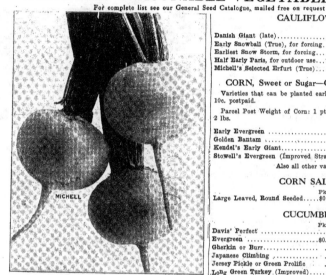

Beet, Crosby's Egyptian

CAULIFLOWER

	Pkt.	¼ oz.	Oz.
Danish Giant (late)	$0.25	$1.25	$4.50
Early Snowball (True), for forcing	.25	1.25	4.50
Earliest Snow Storm, for forcing	.25	1.75	5.00
Half Early Paris, for outdoor use	.10	.50	1.75
Michell's Selected Erfurt (True)	.25	1.25	4.50

CORN, Sweet or Sugar—Connecticut Grown

Varieties that can be planted early in July. Large Packets 10c. postpaid.

Parcel Post Weight of Corn: 1 pt. equals 1 lb.; 1 qt. equals 2 lbs.

	Lb.	5 lbs.
Early Evergreen	$0.35	$1.50
Golden Bantam	.35	1.50
Kendel's Early Giant	.40	1.60
Stowell's Evergreen (Improved Strain)	.35	1.60

Also all other varieties

CORN SALAD

	Pkt.	Oz.	¼ lb.	Lb.
Large Leaved, Round Seeded	$0.10	$0.20	$0.65	$2.25

CUCUMBER

	Pkt.	Oz.	¼ lb.	Lb.
Davis' Perfect				Sold out
Evergreen	$0.10	$0.20	$0.60	$1.75
Gherkin or Burr	.10	.20	.65	2.25
Japanese Climbing	.10	.15	.50	1.75
Jersey Pickle or Green Prolific	.10	.20	.60	1.75
Long Green Turkey (Improved)				Sold out
White-Spined (Arlington Strain)	.10	.20	.60	1.75

ENGLISH CUCUMBERS

These are ideal for growing outdoors as well as under glass. They produce enormous fruits generally 18 to 24 inches long and 3 inches in diameter.

Lockie's Perfection, Sion House, Telegraph, Tender and True. Each per packet of 12 seeds, 30c.; $2.25 per 100 seeds.

CARROTS

	Pkt.	Oz.	¼ lb.	Lb.
Chantenay Half Long	$0.10	$0.15	$0.50	$1.50
Danvers Half Long	.10	.15	.50	1.50
Early Scarlet Horn	.10	.20	.65	2.00
Guerande or Oxheart	.10	.15	.50	1.50
Half Long Scarlet	.10	.20	.65	2.00
Improved Long Orange	.10	.15	.50	1.50
Orange Beauty	.10	.20	.65	2.00
Rubicon Half Long	.10	.15	.50	1.50
Very Early Short Horn	.10	.20	.65	1.75
White Belgian	.10	.20	.50	1.50

ENDIVE

Broad Leaved Batavian (Escarolle)	.10	.20	.60	1.75
Giant Fringed	.10	.20	.60	1.75
Improved Green Curled	.10	.20	.60	1.75
White Curled (self blanching)	.10	.20	.60	1.75

KALE

Dwarf Green Curled	.10	.25	.75	2.75
Imperial Long Standing	.10	.25	.65	2.00

BEET—Table Varieties

	Pkt.	Oz.	¼ lb.	Lb.
Arlington Favorite Blood (Turnip)	$0.10	$0.20	$0.60	$2.00
Bassano Extra Early (Turnip)	.10		.60	2.00
Bastian's Extra Early (Turnip)	.10	.20	.50	1.75
Bastian's Half Long Blood	.10		.50	1.75
Crimson Globe (Michell's Imp'd)	.10	.15	.50	1.75
Crosby's Egyptian (Turnip)	.10	.20	.60	2.00
Detroit Dark Red (Turnip)	.10	.15	.50	1.50
Eclipse Extra Early (Round)	.10	.20	.60	1.75
Edmand's Blood (Turnip)	.10	.20	.60	1.75
Lentz Early	.10	.20		1.75
Michell's Winter Keeper	.10	.25	.85	3.00
Swiss Chard. Giant Lucullus	.10	.20	.65	2.00

BEANS—Green Podded, Dwarf Varieties

Large Packets of all varieties 10c. postpaid. If Beans are wanted by parcel post please add postage.

	Lb.	5 lbs.
Black Valentine	$0.35	$1.60
Boston Navy or Pea (used shelled)	.35	1.45
Early Mohawk (6 weeks)	.35	1.60
Extra Early Refugee	.40	1.75
Full Measure	.35	1.60
Mammoth Stringless	.35	1.60
Red Valentine	.35	1.50
Stringless Forcing	.45	1.75
Stringless Green Pod Improved	.35	1.50
White Marrowfat (used shelled)	.35	1.50

BEANS—Wax or Yellow Podded Dwarf Varieties

	Lb.	5 lbs.
Black or German Wax	$0.35	$1.50
Currie's R. P. Golden Wax	.40	1.50
Dwarf Golden Wax Improved	.40	1.75
Refugee Wax	.40	1.75
Round Podded Kidney Wax	.45	2.15
Sure Crop Stringless Wax	.40	1.75
Wardwell's Kidney Wax	.45	1.90

All Prices Subject to Market Changes

(oe)

Michell's Seasonable Vegetable Seeds, Etc.

LETTUCE

	Pkt.	Oz.	¼ lb.	Lb.
All Heart	$0.10	$0.25	$0.65	$2.00
All-Right (Michell's)	.10	.25	.65	2.00
Black Seeded Simpson (loose leaved)	.10	.20	.60	1.75
Dutch Butter, Private Stock	.10	.20	.60	1.75
Improved Hanson	.10	.20	.60	1.75
Kingsholm Cos or Romaine	.10	.20	.60	1.75
Mammoth Salamander (True)	.10	.20	.60	1.75
May King	.10	.25	.75	2.25
Michell's Number One	.10	.20	.75	2.50
New York or Wonderful	.10	.20	.70	2.00
Silesian, loose leaved	.10	.20	.60	1.75

For other Varieties see our General Seed Book

PARSLEY

	Pkt.	Oz.	¼ lb.	Lb.
Champion Moss Curled	$0.10	$0.15	$0.45	$1.50
Double Curled or Covent Garden	.10	.15	.45	1.50
Hamburg or Rooted	.10	.15	.45	1.50

PEAS

Large Packets of all varieties 10c. postpaid.
Parcel Post Weight of Peas: 1 pt. equals 1 lb.; 1 qt. equals 2 lbs.

	Lb.	5 lbs.
Alaska (Extra Early)	$0.35	$1.50
Bliss, Abundance (Medium Early)	.35	1.60
Dandy Extra Early (Michell's)	.35	1.60
Early June	.35	1.50
Gradus or Prosperity (Extra Early)	.55	2.50
Michell's Special Extra Early	.40	1.80

For other Varieties see our General Seed Book

RADISH

	Pkt.	Oz.	¼ lb.	Lb.
Cardinal Globe (Improved Strain)	$0.10	$0.20	$0.60	$1.75
Celestial or White Chinese (Winter)	.10	.20	.60	1.75
China Rose (Winter)	.10	.20	.60	1.75
French Breakfast	.10	.15	.50	1.50
Half Long Black (Winter)	.10	.15	.50	1.50
Icicle (Improved Strain)	.10	.20	.60	1.75
Long Scarlet Short Top	.10	.20	.60	1.75
Round Red	.10	.20	.60	1.75
Scarlet Turnip, White Tipped	.10	.20	.60	1.75
White Box (Felton's Private Stock)	.10	.20	.60	1.75
White Strasburg (½ long)	.10	.20	.60	1.75

SPINACH

	Pkt.	Oz.	¼ lb.	Lb.
Bloomsdale Savoy (Improved Strain)	$0.10	$0.15	$0.30	$0.75
Long Season	.10	.15	.30	.85
New Zealand	.10	.20	.50	1.75

Michell's (Improved Strain) Cardinal Globe Radish

TOMATOES—Adapted for Forcing

	Pkt.	½ oz.	Oz.
Best of All (Sutton's)	$0.10	$0.30	$0.50
Comet	.10	.30	.50
Eclipse (Sutton's) in original Pkts	.85		
Michell's Crackerjack	.10	.30	.60

TURNIP AND RUTA BAGA

	Pkt.	Oz.	¼ lb.	Lb.
Cow Horn	$0.10	$0.15	$0.40	$1.15
Early Purple Top, Flat	.10	.15	.40	1.25
White Globe (Private Stock)	.10	.15	.50	1.50
Snowball	.10	.15	.40	1.15
Southern Seven Top	.10	.15	.40	1.25
Yellow Aberdeen, Flat	.10	.15	.40	1.25
Yellow Globe, or Amber	.10	.15	.40	1.15
Ruta Baga, Yellow Purple Top (Private Stock)	.10	.15	.45	1.50

MICHELL'S SUPERIOR MUSHROOM SPAWN

If wanted by mail, allow for postage at the rate of 10c. per brick.

BRANDYWINE PURE CULTURE SPAWN

This is an entirely new strain, originating in the section of Pennsylvania that supplies New York and Eastern markets with mushrooms.

Per Brick	$0.35	Per 10 Bricks	$2.75
Per 5 Bricks	1.50	Per 25 Bricks	6.50
		Per 50 Bricks	$12.50

AMERICAN SPORE CULTURE SPAWN.

This type produces larger mushrooms than the English, coming into bearing somewhat earlier, and continuing to crop for a long time.

Direct No. 8. Cream White. For use from April to October.
Direct No. 9. Pure White. For use from October to April.

Per Brick	$0.35	Per 10 Bricks	$2.75
Per 5 Bricks	1.50	Per 25 Bricks	6.50
		Per 50 Bricks	$12.50

MICHELL'S SUPERIOR MUSHROOM SPAWN

MICHELL'S RELIABLE GRASS SEEDS

All Prices subject to Market Changes

Possibly no one in the United States specializes more in grass seeds for lawns, pleasure grounds, golf courses, putting greens, pasture and hay fields than we. Our purchases in this commodity direct from the growers at home and Europe amount to many thousand pounds annually. Our grass seeds are rigidly tested for purity and germination at the growing point, in the laboratories of the United States Department of Agriculture and by ourselves, and will be found of highest average. We make special formulas to suit various soils, climatic and local conditions. Our grass mixtures as sold have been based on many tests and on years of careful study, they are properly blended and will give splendid satisfaction. Our grass seed sales, amounting to more than a half million (500,000) pounds per year, enable us to get the choice of the Grass Seed Market.

Quantity to sow for Lawns. You cannot sow too much, the more the better, it means a quicker, more satisfactory and lasting result. We recommend, on new ground, for average mixtures, to sow as follows: One quart on 100 sq. feet (10x10); 4 qts. on 600 feet (20x30); 1 peck on 1500 sq. feet (30x50); 1 bushel on 7000 sq. feet (70x100); 6 to 8 bushels per acre for best effects.

MIXTURES FOR LAWNS

Michell's Clover Lawn Grass. The increasing demand for a grass seed mixture, containing a larger proportion of White Lawn Clover, induced us to offer this brand. After extensive trials we have produced a mixture of grasses, mixed with a most liberal quantity of best recleaned white clover. Especially suited to take firm hold and grow quickly on hard, worn out or burned spots; splendid for seashore lawns. Pint, 30c.; 50c. per qt.; 2 qts., 90c.; $1.75 for 4 qts.; peck, $3.00; $12.00 per bush. (30 lbs.); 100 lb. lots and over, 37½c. per lb.

Michell's Top Notch. The best Lawn Mixture in existence, and can justly be called the top-notch of quality. It is a perfectly blended combination of quick growing, very compact, fine bladed grasses, that will produce a perfect lasting turf in a few weeks. Peck, $2.25; $4.25 per ½ bush.; bush. (25 lbs), $8.00; 100 lb. lots and over, 31c. per lb.

Michell's Green Velvet. Produces a perfect lawn in 4 to 5 weeks' time. Pint, 20c.; 30c. per qt.; 2 qts., 50c.; 90c. for 4 qts.; peck, $1.50; $6.00 per bush. (20 lbs.); 100 lb. lots and over, 28¾c. per lb.

Michell's Evergreen. The standard Lawn Mixture in the United States. Pint, 15c.; 25c. per qt.; 2 qts., 45c.; 75c. for 4 qts.; peck, $1.35; $5.00 per bush. (20 lbs.); 100 lb. lots and over, 24c. per lb.

Michell's Shaded Lawn Grass. Will produce perfect swards in the most densely shaded places. Pint, 20c.; 30c. per qt.; 2 qts., 55c.; $1.00 for 4 qts.; peck, $1.75; $6.50 per bush. (20 lbs.); 100 lb. lots and over, 30c. per lb.

Fairmount Park Lawn Seed. Sow 4 bu. to the acre. Qt., 20c.; 55c. for 2 qts.; 4 qts., 65c.; $1.00 per peck; bush. (15 lbs.), $3.75; 100 lb. lots and over, 22c. per lb.

Michell's Seashore Formula Grass Seed. Contains such grasses as thrive in salt air regions. Sow 4 bu. to the acre. Pint, 20c.; 30c. per qt.; 2 qts., 55c.; $1.00 for 4 qts.; peck, $1.75; $6.50 per bush. (20 lbs.); 100 lb. lots and over, 30c. per lb.

Michell's Terrace or Embankment Grass Seed. Sow 4 bu. to the acre. Qt., 30c.; 55c. for 2 qts.; 4 qts., $1.00; $1.75 per peck; bush. (20 lbs.), $6.50; 100 lb. lots and over, 30c. per lb.

MIXTURES FOR LAWNS (Continued)

Southern States Lawn Grass Seed. Made up especially for dry, hot localities, especially suited to the Southern States. Qt., 25c.; 45c. for 2 qts.; 4 qts., 75c.; $1.25 per peck; bush. (15 lbs.), $4.50; 100 lb. lots and over, 28c. per lb.

Special Sod Grass Seed. Producing a heavy sod in a short time. Qt., 25c.; 45c. for 2 qts.; 4 qts., 75c.; $1.25 per peck; bush. (15 lbs.), $4.50; 100 lb. lots and over, 27½c. per lb.

Woodlands Lawn Mixture. For sowing in dense shade among trees, in woods, etc. Qt., 30c.; 60c. per 2 qts.; 4 qts., $1.10; $2.00 per peck; bush. (20 lbs.), $7.00; 100 lb. lots and over, 32c. per lb.

MIXTURES FOR PLEASURE GROUNDS

Michell's Fair Greens Mixture Golf Course. Composed of short-growing, deep-rooted varieties, resisting plenty of wear. Golf courses, to retain their permanency, should receive additional sowings during the season. Sow 6 bu. per acre. Qt., 30c.; 50c. for 2 qts.; 4 qts., 85c.; $1.60 per peck; bush. (20 lbs.), $6.00; 100 lb. lots and over, 27½c. per lb.

Michell's Putting Greens Mixture. A quick-growing mixture of short, thin-bladed grasses, over which the ball can roll without resistance. We do not recommend less than 50 to 75 lbs. to a green 75 feet square. Qt., 50c.; $1.75 for 4 qts.; peck, $3.25; $12.00 per bush. (25 lbs.); 100 lb. lots and over, 45c. per lb.

Michell's Teeing Grounds Mixture. Used on golf courses or in places where a tough, resisting turf is wanted. Qt., 25c.; 45c. for 2 qts.; 4 qts., 85c.; $1.60 per peck; bush. (20 lbs.), $6.00; 100 lb. lots and over, 27½c. per lb.

Michell's Tennis Court Grass Seed. Tennis courts need grasses of a hardy nature, of fine leaf and close, compact growth. Our mixture will be found particularly adapted for the purpose. Qt., 30c.; 50c. for 2 qts.; 4 qts., 85c.; $1.60 per peck; bush. (20 lbs.), $6.00; 100 lb. lots and over, 27½c. per lb.

Expert Information on Grasses Given Free, either in Person or by Letter. (oe)

GRASSES IN SEPARATE VARIETIES

All Strictly Recleaned and Carefully Tested for Purity and Germination

Prices Subject to Market Changes

We handle the best recleaned grass seeds in separate varieties. Some persons like to do their own mixing or prefer to sow only one kind of grass; we make no charge for mixing.

Lbs. per Bush.	Lb.	Bush.	100 lbs.
35 Bermuda Grass	$1.10		
14 Blue Grass (Kentucky). Extra fancy 3 to 5 bu. per acre ($1.50 per peck)	.50	$5.60	$35.00
14 Blue Grass (Canadian). 3 to 5 bu. per acre	.30	3.50	22.50
20 Creeping Bent. 4 bu. per acre	1.10		
21 Crested Dogstail. 3½ to 4 bu. per acre	.60	10.50	45.00
24 English Rye (Pacey's Fancy Short Seeded). Fine for Lawns. 3 bu. per acre	.30	6.50	22.00
14 Fine Leaved Fescue	1.00		
32 Herd or Red Top. Fancy recleaned, 25 lbs. per acre	.40	10.35	35.00
10 Herd or Red Top. Unhulled, 4 to 5 bu. per acre	.20	1.75	15.00
12 Hard Fescue. ½ bu. per acre	Price on application		
18 Italian Rye. 50 lbs. per acre	.30	5.00	22.50
22 Meadow Fescue. English Blue Grass	.50	10.00	42.50
14 Orchard. 40 lbs. per acre	.50	6.25	40.00
14 Red or Creeping Fescue	.50	6.25	45.00
14 Rhode Island Bent. 40 lbs. per acre	1.10		
12 Sheep's Fescue. 40 lbs. per acre	.45	5.75	40.00
— Sudan Grass	Price on application		
— Sweet Vernal (Perennial). 3 lbs. per acre with other grass	Price on application		
— Sweet Vernal (Annual). 5 lbs. per acre with other grass	Price on application		
10 Tall Meadow Oat (French Rye Grass).	.50	4.75	45.00
45 Timothy Seed. ½ bu. per acre alone	Price on application		
14 Wood Meadow. 30 lbs. per acre	.75	9.80	67.50

WESTERNWOLTH'S RYE GRASS

A New Forage and Pasture Grass of Extraordinary Productiveness

This new grass was discovered in Holland in 1906. It has been tried out in various parts of Europe with splendid results. It surpasses the Italian Rye Grass in rapidity of growth and tonnage; on average soil, top dressed with Nitrate of Soda, it will yield five or six cuttings a year. It is a splendid grass mixed with Red Clover for hay or pasture, or for a quick supply of green food for horses and cows. Its germination is high and the quality of the feed is strictly A1. Seed sown in Europe, April 20th, was in full flower head June 25th. Our stock has been procured from the introducer, and we take pleasure in recommending it as one of the best forage plants. The full grown height is about 3½ feet; it is hardy and when sown will last quite a while. It requires 75 lbs. to properly sow an acre. 40c. per lb.; bush. (24 lbs.); $8.40; $27.50 per 100 lbs.

(oe)

MIXTURES FOR MISCELLANEOUS PURPOSES

Michell's Permanent Pasture Grass Seed. The old prevalent method of sowing timothy and clover, has been found not only costly, but too short-lived to answer the purpose. The old custom has given way to the new, which is the sowing of a mixture of permanent grasses. Michell's Permanent Pasture Grass Seed is composed of about 10 of the best growing and most nutritious grasses and clovers for stock feeding or grazing. One sowing will last many years, although we advise additional sowing each autumn, just previous to which a light harrowing is recommended to give the grass a quick hold. Sow 3 to 4 bu. per acre on new land or 2 bu. on established pastures. Per qt., 25c.; 75c. per 4 qts.; peck, $1.25; $4.50 per bush. (20 lbs.); 100 lb. lots or over, 20c. per lb.

Michell's Permanent Hayfield Grass Seed. While timothy is still extensively sown for this purpose, this mixture is gradually being adopted by the progressive farmer. Its main advantages are that certain grasses in this mixture will grow better in varying conditions of soil, thus giving a full crop of hay on land that otherwise might produce but a half crop of timothy and clover. Our formula is the outcome of thorough trials in every kind of soil. Sow 3 to 4 bu. per acre on new lands or 2 bu. on established fields. Per qt., 25c.; 75c. per 4 qts.; peck, $1.25; $4.50 per bush. (20 lbs.); 100 lb. lots or over, 20c. per lb.

Michell's Poultry Yard Grass Seed. Chickens love grass and should be placed where they can get it as much as possible. We put plenty of clover seed in this mixture, as it is very nutritious and the fowls relish it. Per qt., 25c.; 40c. per 2 qts.; 4 qts., 75c.; $1.25 per peck; bush. (15 lbs.), $4.50; 100 lb. lots or over, 27c. per lb.

WHITE CLOVER

Choice recleaned for sowing on lawns, pastures, etc. Sow 10 to 12 lbs. per acre. Per oz., 10c; 25c. per ¼ lb.; ½ lb., 45c.; 85c. per lb.; 5 lbs. for $4.25; $8.00 per 10 lbs.; bush. (60 lbs.), $43.00; $75.00 per 100 lbs.

PRICES ON GRASSES SUBJECT TO MARKET CHANGES

Note—If grasses are wanted by parcel post, allow for postage when remitting.

PRICES SUBJECT TO MARKET CHANGES

Alfalfa, or Lucerne (Medicago Sativa). The most valuable forage crop on the American farm today, and can be truly termed a mortgage lifter. It is sown during May, August and September. Our special Circular on Alfalfa explains this fully, and is free for the asking. Sow not less than ½ bushel (30 lbs.) per acre, preferably with no other crop. Our seed is always over 99 per cent. pure, and will invariably give the best of results. Choice Non-Irrigated Western Grown Seed. Price on application.

Grimm Alfalfa. Claimed to be hardy in any and all regions, a heavy yielder and of deeper rooting ability. Highly recommended by various State Experiment Stations. It requires only about 10 lbs. of Grimm Alfalfa to properly seed an acre, on account of its great root system and spreading habit. Price on application.

Alsike, or Swedish Clover (Trifolium Hybridum). One of the best for mixing with timothy; it is perfectly hardy in every climate or soil condition and seldom has to be reseeded. Under ordinary conditions it grows from 1 to 2 feet high; is sown early in the spring or late summer and early autumn. It is as nutritious as red clover and is rapidly coming to the front as a valuable farm crop. The flower resembles the white clover except that the head is larger and has a red tinge on the edge. Sow 10 to 15 lbs. per acre alone, or 8 lbs. per acre with timothy. Price on application.

Bokhara or Sweet Clover (Melilotus Alba). While extensively used as a bee food, this is a valuable variety for soiling (green manure). It grows from 3 to 5 feet high, according to soil and location; can be cut as often as three times in a season if wanted for forage. Sow 15 lbs. per acre in early spring, alone, or 10 lbs. per acre with other crops. We handle only the true white flowering hardy variety. Choice Hulled Seed. Price on application.

Crimson Clover (Trifolium Incarnatum). This is used principally for soiling or green manuring, for which purposes it is highly valuable. If desired for feed, cut it just before it flowers. When desired for green manure, it should be allowed to mature; its height is from 1 to 2 feet. Sow any time from April to October, the earlier the better, 20 lbs. to the acre. If sown in early spring it can be plowed down the first year. Late summer or fall seeding is usually practiced. It is not hardy for more than one season and must be sown each year. Price on application.

Mammoth Red Clover (Trifolium Pratense Perenne). Sometimes called Sapling or Pea Vine Clover and English Cow Grass. This differs from the "Medium," being of a ranker growth and yielding more fodder per acre. It ripens somewhat later and is more hardy, lasting several seasons longer than the medium red clover. It also does well on poorer soils. The seed cannot be distinguished from the former. Our supply, however, is strictly reliable. Sow in early spring or in July and August, using 20 lbs. per acre alone, or with other crops 10 lbs. per acre; flowers pink. It can be cut several times in a season. Price on application.

Our Strains of Red Clover are unusually fine

Red Clover, Medium (Trifolium Pratense). More widely known and used than any other; used principally for hay purposes. Height from 18 inches to 2½ feet. Sow early in the spring or in late summer—July and August; if alone, 20 lbs. per acre; if with other crops, 10 lbs. per acre. A red clover field can usually be cut twice in a season. It is not hardy for a period of years, being usually resown every third season; flowers pink. Price on application.

White Dutch or Lawn Clover (Trifolium Repens). This is valuable for pasturage as well as for lawns; it succeeds where other clovers and grasses fail, and it seldom dies out. It can be sown at all seasons; flowers greenish white. Sow 10 to 12 lbs. per acre if alone, or 5 lbs. if sown on old turf or with other crops. 10c. per oz.; ¼ lb., 25c.; 45c. per ½ lb.; 85c. lb.; $4.25 per 5 lbs.; 10 lbs., $8.00; $43.00 per bu. of 60 lbs.; per 100 lbs., $75.00. Prices on White Clover subject to change.

BEANS, SOJA OR SOY

Excellent for green manuring, fodder and silo purposes. Sow 1½ bushels per acre alone, or ½ bushel Soja Beans with one bushel Cow Peas.
Mammoth Yellow (Late).
Wilson (Early). Prices on application.

BUCKWHEAT

In the locality of Philadelphia this is sown any time from June 1st to July 15th; one bushel of 48 lbs. broadcasted to the acre. It makes a very fine quality of flour, but is largely used for poultry food. For planting adjacent to game preserves it provides excellent food for the birds. The flower makes ideal bee food, while the straw is very abundant. Our seed is grown by a specialist in New York State, who procures his seed stock every few years from Japan. Any of the clover crops can be sown with buckwheat, these to mature the following season. Buckwheat frequently yields as much as 80 bushels to the acre.
Japanese. Very early variety. Dark, large grain.
Silver Hull. Late maturing variety; grain making whiter flour; very prolific.
Price of Buckwheat on application.

A Field of Japanese Buckwheat

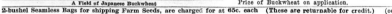

2-bushel Seamless Bags for shipping Farm Seeds, are charged for at 65c. each   **(These are returnable for credit.)**   (oe)

BARLEY

The straw is good for green feed or when cured, as hay. The grain in the hull is excellent poultry feed. If wanted for hay it should be cut while the grain-head is in a soft or milky condition. Sow broadcast 1½ to 2 bushels per acre from May 15th to July 1st. 48 lbs. per bushel.

Barley makes an ideal nurse crop for spring sown Alfalfa. When sown in connection with alfalfa, use ½ to ¾ bushel per acre broadcast; when ripe, harvest as usual or cut and rake off. Beardless. New York grown stock; frequently yields 50 bushels per acre. Price on application.

KAFFIR CORN—White, for Seed

This belongs to the Sugar Cane family and has great drought-resisting qualities; the grain is used for feeding poultry and the fodder for cattle; is ideal for planting where seed corn has failed to germinate and it is too late to replant. Grows from 4 to 6 feet high, the grain being produced on the top of stalk in the shape of a brush; frequently as many as four heads of grain will be found on a single stalk. It usually ripens after the first few frosts; produces enormous crops. Can be sown as late as July at the rate of 10 lbs. per acre in drills. (Bu. 56 lbs.). Price on application.

COW PEAS

Cow Peas are one of the best, largest yielding and most nutritious of the farm crops. Cattle, sheep or hogs can be turned into a field of them and they will eat them greedily, and the stubble can be plowed under. In the latitude of Philadelphia, sow from May 1st to July 1st, two bushels per acre broadcast, or one bushel per acre in drills. For a large crop, sow the seed as late as possible, and not too thick.

Black. One of the popular varieties extensively grown. It is very prolific and matures early. It is of upright growth, consequently preferred for ploughing under or for grazing stock.

Large Black Eye. An exceedingly heavy cropper, but late to mature. In the South the seed of this variety is sold for dried peas for household use; it is claimed they are quite delicious.

Whippoorwill. Medium early; upright growing, a variety more extensively used than any other. The seed is brown and gray speckled. It is a heavy producer of both pods and fodder. Some claim this variety gathers more nitrogen than others.

Prices: These fluctuate constantly; will be quoted on request.

MILLET

Can be sown as late as July 15th and yield a tremendous crop. Is also desirable for green manuring, when it should be turned under when about 10 inches high. It makes an excellent green food for stock not allowed to pasture. If used for hay and dried it should be cut just as it matures.

Hungarian. The seed produces hay not so fine in quality as the "Golden," also fully a foot less in height. It can, however, be sown some 2 weeks later. Sow 1 bushel (50 lbs.) per acre.

Japanese Barnyard. This wonderful Millet yields possibly more fodder than any other forage plant that requires so little to sow an acre. Frequently as high as 12 tons of green food has been obtained from an acre. If sown early in May it may be cut twice in one season. Sow 12 lbs. per acre broadcast; any time from May 1st to June 15th.

Pearl (Pencillaria Spicata). A valuable fodder plant. Enormously productive. Sow in drills 2 feet apart, 10 to 12 lbs. per acre.

Tennessee Golden. This requires a longer season to mature than the other sorts; it produces a very fine quality of hay and makes a larger seed head. In good seasons it grows about 4 ft. high. Sow 1 bu. (50 lbs.) broadcast to the acre, from April 10th to July 10th.

A Head of Japanese Millet

RAPE

Dwarf Essex. An excellent green food for sheep and hogs; can be pastured 8 weeks after sowing. Sow 6 lbs. per acre broadcast or in drills from April 1st to October 1st. It produces enormous crops and is ideal green manure. Price on application.

WINTER RYE

Pennsylvania White. This makes a fine winter cover crop, being usually sown in the autumn as late as November; making a very fine yield of long, stiff straw. Winter rye will not mature if sown in spring. 56 lbs. per bu. Sow 1½ bushels per acre. Price on application.

TIMOTHY SEED

For sowing among wheat as a second year hay crop, or for sowing alone for a first year hay crop, this is extensively used. We aim to sell the purest and highest germinating quality. 45 lbs. per bushel. Samples and quotations on request.

WINTER VETCH (Vicia Villosa)

Sometimes called Sand or Hairy Vetch. Our stock of this is the true type, being imported by us direct from Russia which will absolutely live throughout the winter. Sow from August 1st to October 1st, but the earlier the better, broadcast, 1 bushel per acre, to which we suggest adding a bushel of winter rye or wheat. In the spring it can be plowed under as green manure, or when in flower cut for hay. All stock relish it keenly. Price on application.

WINTER WHEAT (Ready about Sept. 10th)

Four-Rowed Fultz (Bearded). Red.
Fultzo-Mediterranean (Beardless). Red.
Lancaster-Fulcastet (Bearded). Dark Red.
Leap's Prolific (Beardless). Dark Red.
Miracle (Bearded). Red.
Price's Wonder (Bearded). Dark Red.
Price on application.

TRUE WINTER VETCH

2-bushel Seamless Bags for shipping Farm Seeds, are charged at 65c. each. (These are returnable for credit.) (oe)

Planet Jr. Tools

No. 3.	Hill and Drill Seeder....	$21.00
No. 4.	Combined Hill and Drill Seeder, Single Wheel Hoe, Cultivator and Plow (see cut)........	22.50
No. 4D.	Hill and Drill Seeder...	17.75
No. 25.	Combined Hill and Drill Seeder, Double and Single Wheel Hoe and Cultivator	25.50
No. 31.	Combined Drill Seeder and Single Wheel Hoe.	14.50
No. 31D.	Drill Seeder only...	11.50
No. 11.	Double and Single Wheel Hoe, Cultivator, Plow and Rake	18.00
No. 12.	Double Wheel Hoe.....	14.50
No. 16.	Single Wheel Hoe, Cultivator, Rake and Plow.	11.75
No. 17.	Single Wheel Hoe........	9.75
No. 33.	Single Wheel Hoe........	7.25
No. 13.	Double Wheel Hoe.......	10.00
No. 17½.	Single Wheel Hoe.......	8.40
No. 18.	Single Wheel Hoe.......	6.75
No. 14.	Double Wheel Hoe.......	16.00
No. 19.	Garden Plow and Cultivator	6.75
Firefly Garden Plow		4.50
Star Pulverizer		6.60

IRON AGE TOOLS

No. 320.	Single Wheel Hoe......	$10.50
No. 11.	Wheel Plow	5.00
No. 12.	Wheel Hoe and Plow...	5.75
No. 301R.	Double Wheel Hoe:....	12.75
No. 303.	Double Wheel Hoe....	8.50
No. 39.	Hand Plow	3.00
No. 306.	Double and Single Wheel Hoe and Combined Hill and Drill Seeder	20.00
No. 304.	Combined Double and Single Wheel Hoe and Drill Seeder...........	20.00
Gem Single Wheel Hoe...........		8.50
Gem Double Wheel Hoe...........		10.50
Victory Wheel Plow and Cultivator		5.00
Model Seed Drill.................		13.75
No. G5. Fairy Garden Cultivator..		3.00

Michell's Lawn Mowers

THE MICHELL HIGH WHEEL BALL BEARING LAWN MOWER

(5-blade cylinder)

15-inch	....$17.60	19-inch	.....$22.00
17-inch	...... 19.80	21-inch	..... 24.20

PENNA. AND CONTINENTAL

Either at the following prices:

Low wheel, 8-in. diameter (Penna. only).

12-inch	.....$15.00	16-inch	.....$19.00
14-inch	...... 17.00	18-inch	...... 21.00

High wheel, 10½-inch diameter.

15-inch	.....$25.00	19-inch	.....$31.25
17-inch	...... 28.25	21-inch	..... 34.75

Note: Continental machines cannot be furnished in low wheel types.

PENNA. JR. BALL BEARING

8-inch or low wheel, 5-blade cylinder, 5½-inch diameter.

12-inch	.....$17.00	16-inch	.....$20.50
14-inch	...... 18.00	18-inch	...... 22.25

10-inch or high wheel, 5-blade cylinder, 6-inch diameter.

15-inch	.....$27.25	19-inch	.....$32.50
17-inch	....: 29.50	21-inch	...... 36.00

PENNSYLVANIA GOLF

9½-inch, high wheel, 7 blades, ball bearing.

12-inch	.....$33.55
19-inch	...... 37.40
21-inch	...... 40.70

PENNA. PUTTING GREENS

12-inch	.....$23.65	16-inch	.....$31.60
14-inch	..... 27.50	18-inch	...... 34.90

TOWNSEND'S GOLF WONDER

14-inch	.....$25.00	20-inch	.....$31.00
16-inch	..... 27.00	22-inch	..... 33.00
18-inch	..... 29.00	24-inch	..... 36.00

Catchers for any of the above, $6.00 each.

THE PULL-EASY WEEDER AND CULTIVATOR

The teeth are adjustable to various widths; splendid for going between rows of young, growing crops. Price, $1.75.

INVINCIBLE CULTIVATOR

For the kitchen garden and truck patch; a useful tool for weeding, loosening the soil, etc. Price, with long handle, $1.25.

Pull-Easy Weeder and Cultivator

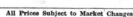

COLDWELL HIGH WHEEL

Ball-bearing, 4-blade cylinder.

14-inch	.....$14.00	18-inch	.....$17.00
16-inch	..... 15.50	20-inch	..... 18.25

GREAT AMERICAN BALL BEARING

High wheel.

15-inch	.....$18.00	19-inch	.....$23.00
17-inch	...... 20.50	21-inch	...... 25.25

PHILADELPHIA MOWERS

High wheel, style A. High wheel, style K.

15-inch	.....$28.00	14-inch	.....$15.50
17-inch	..... 30.75	16-inch	..... 18.00
19-inch	..... 34.00	18-inch	..... 20.25
21-inch	..... 37.50	20-inch	..... 22.50

ORCHID MOWERS

High wheel, ball bearing.

14-inch	.........$13.00
16-inch	.... 14.00
18-inch	.... 15.00

LAWN TRIMMERS

For cutting around walks, drives, flower beds and borders.

Coldwell	.........$ 8.50
Penna. Regular style, plain-bearing.	8.50
Penna. Undercut style, ball-bearing.	12.65
Capitol	.... 8.50
Coldwell Gem, 8-inch cut..........	8.50

GRASS CATCHERS

Braun's Make

For the Pennsylvania, Continental, Great American B. B. and New Departure Mowers.

12-inch	.....$2.50	15-inch	.....$3.00
14-inch	..... 2.75	17-inch	..... 3.00
16-inch	..... 3.00	19-inch	..... 3.25
18-inch	..... 3.00	21-inch	..... 3.50

Catchers for Penna. Golf Mowers All sizes, 14- to 21-inch, $6.00 each.
C tch for Penna. P. G. Mowers. All sizes, 12- to 18-inch, $6.00 each.

K. C. GRASS CATCHER

Fits any Mower

Made of sheet iron bottom and canvas sides. Price, 12- to 16-inch size, $2.00 each; 18- to 22-inch size, $2.25.

HORSE LAWN MOWERS, ETC.

Prices on Application

PLANET JR. CELERY HILLERS

Double, for hilling one side of 2 rows. Price, double style, $37.00.

All Prices Subject to Market Changes

(oe)

McCORMICK MOWING MACHINE
GEAR DRIVE

3½ and 4 ft. cut, vertical bar, 1-horse machine.

4½ and 5 ft. cut (New 4), 2-horse machine.

4½ and 5 ft. cut, vertical bar, 2-horse machine.

Price on application

TENNIS COURT MARKER

Junior Line-o-graph. A perfect liquid lime tennis court marker especially designed for private courts, works perfectly on grass or clay. $30.00 each, F. O. B. factory. F. O. B., Philadelphia, $32.50.

Junior Line-o-graph Tennis Marker

Apollo Lawn Cleaner

APOLLO LAWN CLEANER

For sweeping lawns, paths, putting greens, tennis courts, etc. The revolving brush gathers up the smallest particles, leaving the surface swept very clean. The sweeping area is 28 inches. Price, $20.00.

Pennsylvania Lawn and Putting Green Cleaner

The flexible rake bars are of wood, with steel springs and teeth; they rotate like a lawn mower cylinder and clean up leaves, mown grass, litter or rubbish, throwing it into a receptacle or bag in the rear.

24-in. rake $25.00
Penna. Putting Greens Sweeper, 24-inch, $25.00.
Sweeping Brushes. Can be readily attached to the Rake for sweeping putting greens, paths, etc. $6.00 per set of three.

RUBBISH BASKETS

On all large places, on the lawn or in flower and vegetable gardens, a basket for gathering up rubbish and litter will be found a great convenience, especially when it is suited for the purpose. This basket holds 3 bushels and can be carried or wheeled from place to place on a barrow. Price, with rope handles, $4.25 each.

Rubbish Basket

BARREL TRUCKS, ETC.

The price below includes barrel and truck. The latter is constructed so that the barrel may be detabhed quickly and the leaf rack attached.

1½-inch tire truck, all iron wheels, with barrel..........$22.25
2½-inch tire truck, all iron wheels, with barrel.......... 23.25
3½-inch tire truck, all iron wheels, with barrel.......... 24.25
Extra Barrels, with trunnions, open head................ 8.00

KEYSTONE LEAF RACKS

This device can be used on wheelbarrows with removable sides. Convenient for gathering leaves, cut grass and rubbish. Has a capacity of 10 bushels; made of galvanized wire, bolted to a wooden base. Price, not including wheelbarrow, $7.50.

WIRE LEAF RACKS

Excellent for gathering leaves, litter, grass, etc. They can be attached to a water barrel truck.
Leaf Rack only; no truck................................$13.50
Leaf Rack with 1½-inch tire truck..................... 28.50
Leaf Rack with 2½-inch tire truck..................... 29.50
Leaf Rack with 3½-inch tire truck..................... 30.50

WHEEL BARROWS

The measurements of barrows are understood viz: Length, meaning inside length of body; depth, inside depth at front; width, outside width at handles.

Eastern   Greenhouse   Canal

	No.	Tire In.	Length In.	Depth In.	Width In.	Price
Eastern	3	1½	28	11	22	$ 8.50
Eastern	4	3	26¼	11½	27	10.00
Eastern	5	3	28¼	11¾	27	11.00
Eastern (Boys')	2		21¾	9¼	20	7.75
Canal Side dump (bolted)						7.00

Special Greenhouse Style with narrow body and handle width $15.00

LAWN MOWER OIL

Pure oil that will not gum or get sticky is an essential for the satisfactory operation of every mower. The oil sold by us has been selected with this point in view.
Prices: Per pint, 40c.; 60c. per quart; per ½ gal., 75c.; $1.25 per gal.; 5 gals., $4.50.
Lawn Mower Oil cannot be mailed.

GEM OIL CANS

Finished, Brazed Steel.

	Capacity	Spout.	Price.
No. 1706.	8-oz.	6-in. (bent)	$0.60
No. 1706.	8-oz.	6-in. (straight)	.60
No. C14AA.	8-oz.	5-in. (straight), Coppered	.75
No. 1606.	½ pt. 6-in. (bent), Steel		.60
No. 1606B.	½-pt. 6-in. (bent), Brass		1.00

EMERY

For sharpening Lawn Mowers. Price, 25c. per lb.; 10 lbs., $2.35.

SCYTHES

Little Giant

Little Giant, 32-inch........$2.00
Little Giant, 34-inch....... 2.00
Little Giant, 36-inch....... 2.00
Little Giant Brush or Briar 2.00
The Little Giant is the best American-made scythe for field and heavy-grass work.
English, 32-in., rivet back..$2.75
English, 34-in., rivet back.. 2.75
English, 36-in., rivet back.. 3.00
The English Scythes are best for fine grass or lawn work.

Sickles or Grass Hooks

English Rivet Back, No. 2 $1.25
English Solid Back, No. 2.. 1.00
Little Giant .... .75
English Rivet Back.
Soldier Brand
P. P. Wt. 3 lbs. each.   2
No. 2 ....$1.50

SCYTHE STONES

	Each	Doz.
Talacre Style (American)	$0.25	$2.75
Darby Creek	.25	2.75
Carborundum. Very fine	.35	4.00

SCYTHE HANDLES, ETC.

No. 50. Made of hard wood, well finished.
Regular Scythe style.............................$1.75
Snath Clips .... .25

LAWN BORDER SHEARS

Made of finest American steel. They take the place of edging knives, and avoid the necessity of doing much stooping.

Without wheel.
No. 104. 9 in.....$3.25
No. 104. 10 " 3.50
With one wheel.
No. 105. 9 in....$4.00
No. 105. 10 " 4.50

LAWN BORDER SHEARS

For trimming under shrubbery, fences, etc.

No. 1062, 8½-in. blade, long handle, $4.00.

Handles for Border Shears, $1.00 per pair.

GRASS SHEARS

	P.P.Wt.	Each
012.—7 inch, American	2 lbs.	$1.00
3075.—5½ inch, English	2 lbs.	1.50
3075.—6½ inch, English	2 lbs.	1.75
0267.—6 inch, American	2 lbs.	.75

EDGING KNIVES

For trimming edges of paths, etc.

*Equipped with handle. Other styles are sold at additional price of 15c. for handles.

Mehler Edging Tool............$1.25
*No. 040. American 1.00
No. 3863. English, 8 inch........ 2.25
No. 3863. English, 9 inch........ 2.50

PLANET JR. GRASS EDGER

Price, $10.00

Packed weight, 28 lbs.

For stone or cement walks.

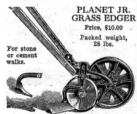

MOLE TRAPS

Reddick Mole Trap

Rittenhouse ..$1.50
Reddick 1.50
P. P. Wt. of the above, 3 lbs.

RUBBISH CONSUMERS

Made of galvanized wire, an indispensable arrangement for burning rubbish, paper, leaves, etc., without endangering property.

Light Wire
No. 1, 20x30 in. $5.50
No. 2, 17x25 in. 4.50
No. 3, 14x21 in. 4.00
No. 4, 12x18 in. 3.50

Extra Heavy Construction
No. 20, 20x30 in. $16

WOODEN RAKES

Ames, No. 37X. 24-tooth, steel bows, for lawns $1.35
Ames, No. 30X. (See cut above). 14-tooth, hard wood bow rake, for hay and field use.................... 1.15
Wire Braced. 20-tooth. Lawn:....... .60

WIRE LAWN OR GRASS RAKE

No.	Tooth		No.	Tooth	
124 R	24..$0.85		36 LR	36..$1.25	
	No. 342 42-tooth,......$1.35				

OLE OLSEN LAWN RAKE

26-tooth, hickory wood. Price, $1.25.

STEEL GRAVEL RAKES

No.	Tooth		No.	Tooth	
G-12	12..$0.95		G 16	16..$1.15	
G 14	14.. 1.05		G 18	18.. 1.25	
	G 20	20-tooth......$1.35			

STEEL BOW RAKES

No.	Tooth		No.	Tooth	
B-12	12..$0.95		B 14	14..$1.05	
B 16	16-tooth......$1.15				

STEEL GARDEN RAKES

No.	Tooth		No.	Tooth	
10	10...$0.85		16	16....$1.00	
12	12.... .90		18	18.... 1.10	
14	14.... .95				

HOE AND RAKE COMBINED

No. 4P. 4-prong...................$0.90
No. 6P. 6-prong................... 1.00

HALF MOON HOES

Best steel, solid sockets, which will not pull out.

No. HM3. 3-inch...................$0.85
No. HM4. 4-inch................... .95
No. HM5. 5-inch................... .95
No. HM6. 6-inch................... 1.00
No. HM7. 7-inch................... 1.00
No. HM8. 8-inch................... 1.05

SQUARE HOES

No. G06. 6-inch, solid shank......$0.90
No. G07. 7-inch, solid shank...... .95
No. G08. 8-inch, solid shank...... 1.00
No. 010. 10-inch, for celery...... 1.50
No. K14½. 14-inch, for celery...... 2.00

TWO-PRONG ONION HOE

Will be found very valuable in weeding in narrow rows.
No. 2P. Price.....................$0.60

WARREN HOES

Excellent tools for making drills preparatory to sowing of seed. The backs can be used for covering.
No. W7......$1.00 No. W8......$1.10

SCUFFLE HOES

Made of best steel.
4-inch	......$1.40	7-in.,	8-in., 10-in.,
5-inch	...... 1.50	Price upon application.	
6-inch	...... 1.60		
Handles for Scuffle Hoes, 15c. each extra.

LAWN GUARDS

For path corners, flower beds, etc. Iron (see cut), nicely painted green, $2.50 each; per doz., $27.00. Not mailable.

Wire, made extra heavy and well galvanized. Price, 35c. each; per doz., $3.50. Not mailable.

LAWN SIGNS

Excellent for putting on grass plots where thoroughfare is not desired.

Iron (shown opposite), painted gray, trimmed red, 85c. each; per doz., $9.00. Parcel post weight, 4 lbs.

KEEP OFF THE GRASS

Enameled Iron Style. (See cut above). The name-plate is finished with green and white enamel, is 20 inches long and about 4 inches wide. Equipped with a substantial iron stake. $1.50 each; per doz., $17.00. Parcel Post Weight, 3 lbs.

All Prices Subject to Market Changes   (oe)

MICHELL'S FARM AND GARDEN TOOLS

STEEL SPADES

Ames $3.00
Portage City 2.00
Nursery (Ames) 3.75
Boys' 1.75

SHOVELS

LONG HANDLE

Ames, round point.................$3.00
Portage City, round point.......... 2.00
Portage City, square point.......... 2.00

SHORT HANDLE

Ames, round point....:.........$3.00
Ames, square point............... 3.00
Portage City, round point.......... 2.00
Portage City, square point.......... 2.00

STEEL SCOOP SHOVELS

All equipped with strapped shanks, wood
D or short handles.
No. 2, 10 -inch mouth..............$1.50
No. 3, 11 -inch mouth.............. 1.75
No. 4, 11½-inch mouth.............. 1.85
No. 5, 12 -inch mouth.............. 1.95
No. 6, 13 -inch mouth.............. 2.00

REDDICK'S POTATO SCOOP

Made of heavy steel wire...........$3.00

SPADING FORKS

Strapped shanks, short or D-wood han-
dle. Made of best quality steel.
No. OHW. Men's, 4-tine $2.00
No. O5HW. Men's, 5-tine 2.25
No. B4D. Boys' or Ladies', 4-tine 1.00
No. EB4. English, heavy tine.... 2.50

MANURE FORKS

Strapped Shanks.

04W—4-tine, light, short handle...$1.75
163 —4-tine, heavy, short handle.. 2.00
05W—5-tine, medium, short handle.. 2.00
06W—6-tine, medium, short handle.. 2.00
044½—4-tine, long handle 1.25
054½—5-tine, long handle 1.50

MANURE DRAGS

For manure, potatoes,
etc. Flat tines.
No. 4BHFM. 4-tine $1.25
No. 6BOH. 6-tine 1.50

GARDEN SETS

For ladies and children, in fact they
are suitable for the country gentleman,
consisting of 1 hoe, 1 rake and 1 spade.
No. 3PF. Large size, per set, $1.50.

STEEL HAY FORKS

No. 026—2-tine, 6-foot handle.......$1.25
No. 036—3-tine, 6-foot handle.......: 1.50

English Digging Fork, No. EB4

The prongs are solid steel, with square
instead of rounded edges, which adapts it
especially for digging in heavy soil, in
which it works with ease. $2.50 each.

BATEMAN FIELD HOE

For digging up stubble, small
stumps, etc.

No. 1. 5½-inch blade, each.........$2.50
No. 2. 6½-inch blade, each......... 2.75
No. 3. 8 -inch blade, each......... 3.00

Eureka Weeding Fork, No. G

Made of best flexible steel; splendid for
loosening soil in the garden, in hotbeds,
etc. 50c. Parcel Post Weight, 2 lbs.

Excelsior Weeding Fork, No. 300

Made of malleable steel, finished in tin.
25c. Parcel Post Weight, 1 lb.

EUREKA WEEDER No. E

Made of flexible steel; very light, an
ideal tool for market gardeners, florists
and amateurs. 50c. Parcel Post Weight,
2 lbs.

EXCELSIOR WEEDER

Made of malleable iron, finished in tin.
25c. Parcel Post Weight, 1 lb.

MAGIC WEEDER

Made of heavy galvanized flexible wire,
with flattened prongs or ends.
Short Handle, Small, 25c.
Short Handle, Medium, 35c.
Long Handle, Large, $1.50.

HAZELTINE HAND WEEDER

No. Bw1, 50c. Parcel Post Weight, 1 lb.

DIBBLES

For Planting Bulbs, Etc.
Equipped with wooden handles.
No. 2180. Brass point, $1.00.
No. 218. Iron point, 70c.
Parcel Post Weight, 1 lb.

D. S. T. Steel Shank Trowel

These are somewhat long in blade and
handle, making a very practical tool. 6-in.
blade. Will last a lifetime. 85c. each.
Parcel Post Weight, 1½ lbs.

Johnson Steel Trowels, No. 211

These are made of one piece steel blade
and shank, equal to the imported trowels.

	P.P.Wt.		P.P.Wt.
5 in......1 lb. $0.75		7 in......1 lb. $0.90
6 in......1 lb. .80		8 in......1 lb. 1.00

Cleves' Angle Trowel, No. 217

For getting dandelion, plantain and
other weeds out of the lawn, and trans-
planting.

	P.P. Wt.	Each.
5 inch...................1 lb.		$0.25
6 inch...................1 lb.		.30
7 inch...................1 lb.		.35

MISCELLANEOUS TROWELS

	P. P. Wt.
No. 213—5 in............½ lb.	$0.20
No. 213—6 in.............½ lb.	.25
Neverbreak—6 in., heavy steel	
1 lb.	.25

POSTHOLE DIGGERS

No. 8. (See cut.)
This bores a hole
3½ ft. deep and can
be adjusted in diam-
eter from 8 to 14
inches. $5.50.
No. 15. Eureka, $2.75

Post Hole Spade.

All steel with either
point or tamper end,
$2.75.

HUSKING PINS

No. 15. Universal.
(See cut.) All metal;
adjustable to any size
hand. 25c.
No. 16. Combina-
tion; leather and
metal. 35c.
Parcel Post Weight,
4 ounces each.

CORN KNIFE

Eureka, bent blade. Weight, 2 lbs...$0.85

BRUSH OR BRIAR HOOK

No. 43. Steel cutting blade; long handle.
Price $1.25

STEEL HEDGE KNIVES

For cutting heavy brush, shrubbery,
hedges, etc. Made of the finest steel with
a slight hook on blade. Each, $2.50.

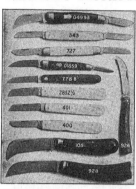

PUTTY DISTRIBUTOR

For distributing putty, mastica, etc.
Price, $1.50. Parcel Post Weight, 1 lb.

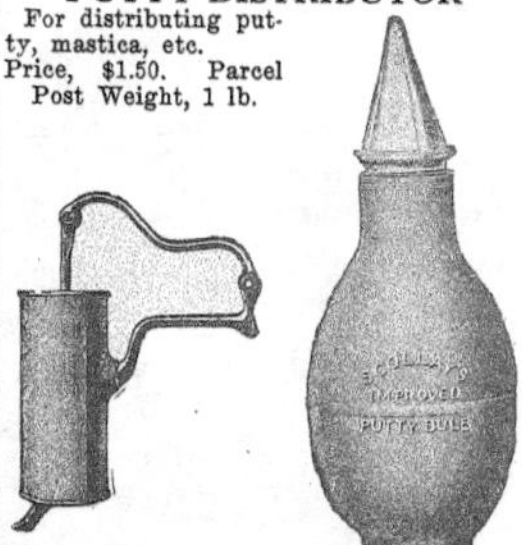

HEDGE SHEARS

	American P.P.Wt.	English Each
107. 6½-inch, Ladies'.4 lbs.	$1.50	....
101. 8-inch ....4 lbs.	2.35	$2.75
101. 9-inch ....5 lbs.	2.65	3.50
101. 10-inch ....5 lbs.	3.00	....
101. 12-inch ....6 lbs.	4.00	....

Bolts and Nuts for hedge shears, 25c. complete.
Handles for Hedge Shears, 75c. per pair.
P. P. Weight on Handles, 2 lbs. per pair.

LOPPING SHEARS

Rhodes' Lopping Shear

No. 109 English, 4-inch cut, finest English steel $7.00
Rhodes. Double cut. Easiest to operate. 24 and 28-inch handles.. 3.50
No. 5400 Clyde, 24 inches long. 1½-inch jaw 4.00
No. 5400 Clyde, 30 inches. Will handle limb 2½-inch diameter..... 4.25
Parcel Post Weight about 5 lbs. each.

GLAZING MATERIALS

Siebert's Glazing Points   Michell's Glazing Points

GLASS CLAMPS

For supporting broken lights of glass.
Per box of 100, $1.75. P. P. Wt., 1¼ lbs.

GLASS CUTTERS

Single Wheel, steel, each............$0.20
6-Wheel, steel, each..:............ .60
Diamond (ebony handle)........... 4.50
Diamond (cocoa handle)........... 5.50

GLAZING POINTS

Michell's Glazing Points. Nos. 2 and 2½, 75c. per 1000. By mail, 85c. per 1000.
Peerless. Three sizes.
No. 1, for single thick glass.
No. 2, for single thick glass.
No. 2½, for double thick glass.
Price, 75c. per 1000. By mail, 10c. per 1000 extra.
Pincers. For driving Michell's and Peerless Points, 60c. By mail, 65c.
Siebert Style. Made with a prominent head; cannot rust; easily driven. ⅝, ¾ and ⅞ inches long. Zinc, 55c. per lb.; 5 lbs., $2.60. 1000 to 1200 in a lb.
Zinc Glazing Nails. 50c. per lb.; 5 lbs., $2.40.

Mastica Machine   Putty Distributor

MASTICA

For glazing greenhouses, new or old.
One gallon will cover about 300 running feet.
1 gallon ....P. P. Wt. 15 lbs. $3.00

MASTICA MACHINE

For distributing mastica, etc. Made of heavy zinc. Price, $2.85. P. P. Wt., 2 lbs.

Permanite Glazing Cement

1 gal.......$2.50 | 5 gal........$11.25

TWEMLOW'S PUTTY

Superior to putty, more easily applied and lasting. Can be put on with a putty bulb or mastica machine.
16-lb. can (1 gal.) P. P. Wt., 18 lbs. $ 3.50
50 lbs. (3 gals.).................. 10.35
80 lbs. (5 gals.).................. 17.00

Hammond's Greenhouse White

A superior white paint. 1 gal., $4.50.

BOSS FRUIT PICKER

Made substantially of galvanized wire.
Can easily be attached to a pole of any length. Price, 50c. P. P. Weight, 2 lbs.

Cider Mill   Wine Press   Grape Grinder

CIDER MILLS

Junior $29.00
Medium 36.00
Senior 47.50
Bantam, single tub........... 22.50

WINE PRESSES

Made of best quality wood, carefully bolted and finished.
No. 1 ....$ 9.75
No. 2 .... 12.00
No. 3 .... 14.50

No. 11 GRAPE GRINDER

Suitable for crushing berries, grapes and similar soft fruit. Price......$5.00

HORTICULTURAL KNIVES

A good knife is an essential to every gardener and florist. Our stock consists of such styles that are practical and in demand. They are all of the best steel. Every one is guaranteed to be perfect and give good satisfaction.

No.	Blades	Style Handle	Each
343	2	Saynor, brass lined, ivory..	$3.50
727W	2	Brass lined, white........	1.40
04993	2	Steel lined, ebony........	1.50
400	1	Saynor, not lined, ivory...	3.25
401	1	Saynor, not lined, ivory...	3.25
2852½	1	Not lined, bone.......:.	1.25
928	1	English, steel lined, stag..	3.00
924	1	English, steel lined, stag.:	2.25
778B	1	Brass lined, ebony........	1.00
105	1	Heavy, steel lined, cocoa..	1.00
303	2	Saynor Pruning, stag.....	2.25
187		Saynor Pruning, 1 blade..	3.00
204B		Saynor Budding, 1 blade:...	4.25

PRUNING SHEARS, ETC.

Our pruning shears are procured from the most reliable makers in America and all are fully guaranteed.

Wiss Pruning Shears

No.		P. P. Wt.	Each
109 Wiss, 8 in. ....:.	2 lbs.		$4.25
60 Pexto American, 9 in..2 lbs.			1.50
65 Pexto American, 9 in..2 lbs.			2.00
R165 Pexto American, 9 in..2 lbs.			2.25
R170 Pexto American, 9 in..2 lbs.			2.50
14 Nickeled, 6½ in....1½ lbs.			1.40
0 American			.60
23 Levin Pruner			1.25

Spiral Springs for any of the above Pruning Shears. 15c. each; per doz., $1.50.
Parcel Post Weight, per doz., ½ lb.

FRENCH PRUNING SHEARS

These have a distinct, very easy working spring and are desirable for one whose hand is liable to fatigue.
No. 1542. 7 inch.................$2.00
No. 1542. 8½ inch................ 2.50
Parcel Post Weight, 2 lbs.
Springs for French Pruning Shears, 35c.

All Prices Subject to Market Changes

(oe)

HOSE

Our stock of this is unusually reliable. Our very large sales enable us to deal direct with the factory, where we obtain lowest prices, which we in turn give our customers the benefit of. Sections of hose in lengths of 25 feet and upward coupled free, smaller sections, couplings, attached, 35c. per pair.

PAT'D. SEPT. 22.96.
Cooper Hose Mender

HOSE MENDERS

	P. P. Weight Doz.	Each.	Doz.
Cooper's ¾-inch	1¼ lbs.	$0.10	$1.00
Cooper's ⅝-inch	1 lb.	.10	1.00
Cooper's ½-inch	1 lb.	.10	1.00
Iron, ¾-inch	2¼ lbs.	.10	1.00
Hudson's ¾-inch (brass),	½ lb.	.08	.85
Hudson's ½-inch (brass),	6 ozs.	.07	.75

THE PERFECT HOSE MENDER

Made entirely of brass, with swivel motion — No band required. For ¾-inch hose, 15c. each; doz., $1.50.
Parcel Post Weight, per doz., 1¾ lbs.

HOSE MENDED.

HOSE.
TUBE.
BAND
PAT'D.
MAY 7th
1889.

HOSE MENDING OUTFIT

(For ¾-inch Hose)

Furnishes a complete outfit, consisting of 6 menders or connections, 18 bands or fasteners, and a pair of pliers for fastening bands. Price, 85c. each. Parcel Post Wt., 1 lb.

RUBBER HOSE

Special attention is called to "Empire Red" Hose, a new brand which, having been thoroughly tried out, has made good.

	Wt. per Ft.	Ft.
*Michell's Special, ½ in.	4 ozs.	$0.18
*Michell's Special, ¾ in.	5 ozs.	.22
*Electric, ¾ in.	5 ozs.	.23
*Electric, ½ in.	4 ozs.	.21
*Revero, ¾ in.	5 ozs.	.22
*Revero, ½ in.	4 ozs.	.19
*Empire Red (Corrugated) ¾ in.		.24
Bull Dog, ⅝ in., 7 ply	5 ozs.	.17½
Spray Pump Hose, ⅜ in.	3 ozs.	.15

P. S.—Brands marked * come in reels of 500 feet and sections in any length to that number of feet may be had.

25- and 50-foot sections of hose coupled free. Smaller sections coupled at the rate of 35c. per pair for couplings attached.

Hose Washers. For inside and outside of coupling: 1 inch, 15c. per doz.; ¼ lb., 50c.; ¾ inch, 10c. per doz.; ¼ lb., 35c.

Caldwell Band as applied to Hose

SURE GRIP

HOSE BANDS

For fastening couplings and menders.

CALDWELL'S

No.		Doz.	100
8.	For 3-ply hose	$0.40	$2.75
6.	For 4-ply hose	.40	2.75

Parcel Post Wt., doz., ¼ lb.; 100, 2¼ lbs.

HUDSON'S

See illustration in Hudson Hose Mender Outfit cut opposite.

	Doz.	100
¾-inch	$0.18	$1.25
½-inch	.18	1.25

Parcel Post Wt., doz., ¼ lb.; 100, 2¼ lbs.

SURE GRIP

¾-inch, 6c. each; per doz., 50c.
Parcel Post Wt., doz., 1 lb.; 100, 9½ lbs.

HOSE COUPLINGS

	P. P. Weight Doz.	Pair.	Doz.
Regular, ½ inch (See cut)	3¼ lbs.	$0.30	$3.00
Regular, ¾ inch	4 lbs.	.30	3.00

Perfect Hose Coupling, ¾-inch, 30c. each; doz., $3.25.

PATENTED IN UNITED STATES
AND FOREIGN COUNTRIES
No. 2 Snap Coupling. No. 1 Snap Coupling

SNAP HOSE COUPLING

Snap Couplings are entirely new and novel. They couple hose instantly, work on a spring, and are water-tight. 35c. pair; doz. pairs, $4.00. (Washers, 20c. doz.)
Parcel Post Weight, per doz., 2½ lbs.

SNAP COUPLING PARTS

No. 2. Male. 15c. each; per doz., $1.50.
Parcel Post Weight, per doz., 1¼ lbs.
No. 1. Female. 25c. each; per doz., $2.50.
Parcel Post Weight, per doz., 1¼ lbs.

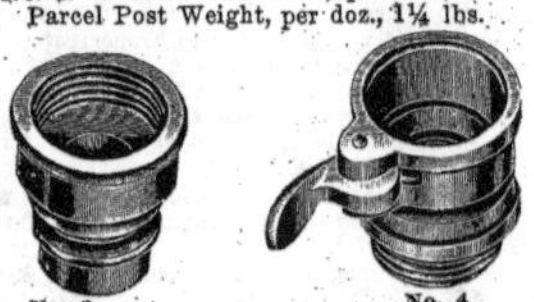
No. 3 No. 4

ACME HOSE COUPLINGS

For quickly connecting and detaching hose.

No. 3 part, for attaching to spigot, 30c. each; doz., $3.00. Weight, per doz., 3 lbs.

No. 4 part, for attaching to hose, 50c. each; doz., $5.00. Weight, doz., 3 lbs.

Couplings complete, consisting of one No. 3 and one No. 4 part, 80c. each; per doz., $8.00. Weight, per doz., 6 lbs.

HOSE REELS

Reels are not mailable.

WIRT'S (All Iron)

No.		
10	100 ft.	$6.50
20	150 ft.	7.00
30	400 ft.	10.50

Victor holds 100 ft. ¾-in. hose. See cut. $4.00.

Victor Reel

NOZZLE HOLDERS

For sticking in the ground while one continues with other work. Made of galvanized heavy wire. Price, 25c. each.
P. P. Wt., 8 ozs.

Note.—If goods are desired by Parcel Post allow for postage on weights stated.

No. 68 SIAMESE HOSE CONNECTION

This permits one lead of hose to be diverted in two directions. Additional three-way connections can be used, according to the water pressure. It is specially adapted for lawn sprinkling. Price, 75c. each.

Parcel Post Weight, 1 lb.

LAWN SPRINKLERS

The Binks Nozzle

Made of aluminum, with brass face; equipped with interchangeable sprays, coarse and fine. It makes watering possible without wetting the hands. Positively the best and most indestructible nozzle made. $3.25 each; worth twice the price. Parcel Post Weight, 1¼ lbs.

Please Note.—Nozzle as now made has a shorter hand grip than illustration shows.

Hose Reducers

For reducing 1-in. pipe to fit regular ¾-in. hose. Each ....75c.

Parcel Post Weight, 1½ lbs.

Hydrant Attachments

To be used for attaching hose to smooth faucets.

No. 2. For small spigot, 55c.
No. 3. For large or standard spigot, 60c.

Parcel Post Weight, ½ lb. each.

	Weight. Price.
Enterprise. No. 1. See cut.	14 lbs. $6.00
Ring. Large, see cut	1 lb. 1.00
Ring or Fountain. Small	¾ lb. .60
Pluvius. 11 in. high	3¼ lbs. 1.75

WATER CANS
(Wotherspoon's)

Extra heavy, with long spout. Will last for years.

Each Wotherspoon can comes equipped with two roses, one coarse and one fine. These cans not mailable.

2 quart (equipped with one rose only), $2.00.

	Round.	Oval.
4 quart	$3.50	.....
6 quart	3.75	$4.00
8 quart	4.00	4.25
10 quart	4.25	4.50
12 quart	4.50	4.75
16 quart	4.75	5.25

12 quart Manure Watering Can 4.75
4 quart Fern or Low Watering Can 2.50

EXTRA ROSES OR SPRAYS

For Wotherspoon Watering Can, either coarse or fine, 50c. each.

Parcel Post Weight on roses, 8 ozs.

ENGLISH WATERING CANS

Made of very heavy tin; carefully enameled inside and out; finished light green.
No. 2, 4 qt....$3.50 | No. 3, 6 qt....$4.50
No. 4, 8 qt.... 4.00 | No. 5, 10 qt.... 4.75

English Watering Cans are not mailable.

GALVANIZED WATER CANS

Fine for cemetery purposes and other places where a can is desired to last several seasons. (Not mailable.)

4 quart	$1.00	12 quart	$1.75
6 quart	1.15	16 quart	1.85
8 quart	1.35	20 quart	2.25
10 quart	1.60		

RUBBER APRONS

For protecting the clothing while watering or doing any work in the garden where your clothes could become soiled. $3.50.

TURBO SPRINKLERS

Especially designed for putting greens and for golf course fairways. Price, $18.

PEACOCK SPRINKLERS

A pipe arrangement, equipped with nozzles set at various distances.
8 ft. Junior..$9.00 | 12 ft. Peacock $16.50

BOSTON SPRAY NOZZLES

These render the same service as does the rose of a watering can. They are screwed on the end of the hose like any other nozzle. Coarse and fine, for ¾-inch hose.

	P.P.Wt.	Price.
Light Copper	½ lb.	$1.00
Heavy Brass	½ lb.	1.50

MYSTIC HOSE NOZZLE

¾-inch hose. Can be regulated to give three different streams. Price, 60c.

Parcel Post Weight, ½ lb.

CHAMPION HOSE NOZZLE

A real champion for results; made of brass, with an adjustable feature that furnishes either a solid stream or a spray in varied degrees of fineness. Price, 85c.

RAINBOW NOZZLE

An all-brass device with an adjustable arrangement, which regulates in a perfect manner the character of the stream this nozzle will throw. Florists consider it one of the very best on the market today. For ¾-inch hose. Weight, 1 lb. Price, $2.25.

Binks Rainfall Sprinkler

A splendid sprinkler that operates on a ball bearing, requiring very little pressure. $1.75 each.

	Weight. Price.
Universal. No. 65. 10 in. high.	4¼ lbs. $2.50
Eureka. No. 55. 10 in. high.	3 lbs. 1.75
Aetna. 24 in. high	6¼ lbs. 2.50
8-Arm Peck	6.00

Crescent Sprinkler

(See cut.) All brass, suitable for watering confined areas, such as side yards, etc. Sprays only a ½ circle at a time. Price, 75c. P.P. Wt., 2 lbs.

	Weight. Price.
Mayflower. 9½ in. high	3½ lbs. $1.75
Preston. 5½ in. high	3½ lbs. 1.75
Waterwitch. 8¾ in. high	1 lb. .60
C.B.G. For golf links	¾ lb. .60

Campbell's Cico Sprinkler

Operates under a reasonable pressure, as there is nothing to revolve, except the water motor, which is a part thereof. This is one of the most recent important improvements in the way of lawn sprinklers. Price, $15.00.

All Prices Subject to Market Changes

(oe)

MICHELL'S PLANT STAKES, WIRE, ETC.

TINNED WIRE

Used for bunching celery, etc.
No. 19, in 10-lb. boxes, cut 8½ inches, 30c. per lb.; per box, $2.75.

CUT BOUQUET WIRE

For Stemming Flowers

Cut 9, 12 or 18 inches in length.

No. 20, 30c. per lb.; per box, 12 lbs., $3.00
No. 22, 32c. per lb.; per box, 12 lbs., 3.25
No. 24, 35c. per lb.; per box, 12 lbs., 3.50

RAFFIA

For tying, basket making and fancy work; very long and fibrous.

Natural Color, 30c. per lb.; 5 lbs., 27½c. per lb.

Green, $1.00 per lb.; 5 lbs., $4.75.

RAFFIATAPE

This article is made of a composition of paper and linen and is tremendously strong; it is about ⅛ inch wide and is put up in 250-yard bolts or hanks. This is very desirable for tying bouquets, flower boxes or for any other purpose where attractive tying material is desired. Color, Nile green. Parcel Post Weight, per bolt, ½ lb.

Per bolt of 250 yards, $1.25; 6 bolts, $7.00.

TWINES, ETC.

	Ball	Lb.
No. 110. White Cayuga, light	$0.45	$0.85
No. 208. White Cayuga	.45	.85
Jute, 2-ply, 3-ply and 5-ply	.25	.45
Linen Bouquet	.15	1.00
Boston Linen, 2- and 3-ply	.30	.60
Green Sea Island	.20	1.25
Special Thin White Cotton	.20	.90
Tarred. For Mat Making	.40	...
Tarred Sisal. For fodder	...	.35
Binder. 5-lb. balls	1.25	...
Express. Very heavy	.40	...

Green Silkaline. For stringing Smilax and Asparagus, etc. F, fine; FF, medium; FFF, coarse.
Price, per spool, 35c.
Price, per lb. (8 spools) $2.50

Green Linen (substitute for Silkaline). Very similar to the above; fast color.
Price, 40c. per spool; $1.50 per lb.

Smilax Twine. Similar to Silkaline, in 2-oz. spools. 30c. per spool; lb., $2.00.

BAMBOO POLES

Used extensively for brushing worm casts off Putting Greens, also for staking young trees.

	Each	Doz.	100
14 ft.	$0.45	$4.75	$32.50
20 ft.	.65	7.00	55.00

GALVANIZED WIRE STAKES

No. 10 WIRE, LIGHT

	P. P. Wt. Doz.	Doz.	100	1000
2 feet	1½ lbs.	$0.25	$1.75	$12.50
2½ feet	1½ lbs.	.35	2.00	15.00
3 feet	2 lbs.	.40	2.25	16.50
3½ feet	2¼ lbs.	.45	2.50	18.00
4 feet	2½ lbs.	.50	2.75	20.00
4½ feet	3 lbs.	.55	3.00	23.50
5 feet		.60	3.50	25.50
6 feet		.65	3.50	28.00

No. 8 WIRE, HEAVY

	P. P. Wt. Doz.	Doz.	100	1000
2 feet	2 lbs.	$0.40	$2.50	$20.00
2½ feet	2½ lbs.	.45	3.00	22.50
3 feet	2¾ lbs.	.50	3.25	25.00
3½ feet	3 lbs.	.60	3.50	27.50
4 feet	3½ lbs.	.70	3.75	30.00
4½ feet	4 lbs.	.80	4.00	32.50
5 feet		.90	4.50	37.50
6 feet		1.00	4.75	42.50

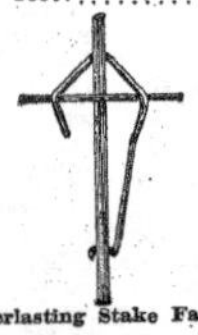

Everlasting Stake Fastener

Wire Stake Tie

WIRE STAKE TIE (Buschardt's)

For fastening plants to stakes, either wire or wood; can be used more than once. 1000 ties in a pkg. (See cut.) Price, $2.50.

STAKE FASTENERS

These take the place of string entirely, lasting several seasons; used for fastening cross wires to galvanized stakes.

	P. P. Wt. per 100	500	1000
Everlasting	½ lb.	$2.25	$4.00
Eureka	¼ lb.	1.35	2.75

WIRE

Allow for postage if wanted by mail.

	Lb.	12-lb. Stone
No. 16. Galvanized	$0.20	$2.00
No. 18. Galvanized	.25	2.25
No. 19. Galvanized	.28	2.50
No. 20. Galvanized	.30	2.75
No. 22. Galvanized	.32	3.00
No. 16. Annealed	.20	1.75
No. 18. Annealed	.22	2.00
No. 20. Annealed	.25	2.25
No. 22. Annealed	.30	2.35
No. 24. Annealed	.35	2.50

GREEN TAPERING STAKES

PAINTED GREEN

	Weight per Doz.	Each.	Doz.	100
1½ feet	½ lb.	$0.03	$0.33	$2.10
2 feet	½ lb.	.05	.55	3.85
2½ feet	1 lb.	.08	.77	5.65
3 feet	1¼ lbs.	.10	1.10	7.45
3½ feet	1½ lbs.	.12	1.32	9.25
4 feet	2 lbs.	.15	1.54	11.00
5 feet		.20	2.00	14.50

ROSE OR DAHLIA STAKES

Round tapering style; painted green.

	Weight per Doz.	Each.	Doz.	100
3 feet	2½ lbs.	$0.15	$1.65	$11.82
3½ feet	4 lbs.	.20	1.98	13.61
4 feet	5 lbs.	.22	2.15	15.67
5 feet		.25	2.64	20.07
6 feet		.30	3.30	24.64

SQUARE PLANT STAKES

These are painted green and nicely tapered and finished.

	Weight per Doz.	Each.	Doz.	100
1½ feet	½ lb.	$0.03	$0.25	$1.85
2 feet	½ lb.	.04	.40	2.75
2½ feet	1 lb.	.05	.56	4.00
3 feet	2 lbs.	.10	1.00	7.00
3½ feet	2½ lbs.	.12	1.15	8.00
4 feet	4 lbs.	.14	1.25	9.50
5 feet		.18	1.85	14.00
6 feet		.25	2.75	16.00

CANE STAKES

	Doz.	100	250	1000
Southern, 7 to 8 ft.	$0.35	$2.00	$3.75	$14.00

JAPANESE GREEN CANE STAKES

These are very attractive for all purposes of plant staking; thin and very strong.

	Doz.	100	250	1000
1½ feet	$0.15	$0.75	$3.25	$6.00
2 feet	.20	1.25	5.50	10.00
2½ feet	.25	1.35	6.75	12.00
3 feet	.30	1.50	7.75	14.00
3½ feet	.35	2.00	8.50	16.00
4 feet	.40	2.25	9.50	18.00

JAPANESE NATURAL CANE STAKES

	Doz.	100	500	1000
2½ feet	$0.20	$1.35	$5.75	$10.60
3 feet	.25	1.60	7.00	12.50
4 feet	.30	2.00	8.00	15.00
5 feet	.35	2.20	9.25	17.50
6 feet	.40	2.35	11.00	20.00

HYACINTH STAKES

Used for staking hyacinths, tulips and slender plants; dyed green.

	P. P. Wt. per 100	Doz.	100	1000
5 inch	1½ lbs.	$0.05	$0.20	$1.50
12 inch	2 lbs.	.07	.30	2.50
18 inch	2 lbs.	.10	.40	3.50

THE KEY DUSTER GUN

This device introduces, or rather makes more practical, the application of dry powder as an insecticide or fungicide. It contains a chamber into which is inserted a cartridge or canister of powdered insecticide, referred to below. When the cartridge or canister of insecticide is inserted, the gun opens it automatically, while it may be removed without loss of material, thus enabling the operator to change from one preparation to the other.

The new, quick and easy way of using insecticides and fungicides in the cartridge. Killing many bugs; preventing certain blights.

The following is a list of preparations packed in form suitable for use in the Key Gun:

	Price per canister
Bordeaux Arsenate	$0.15
Lime Sulphur	.15
Hellebore	.20
Price of Gun	3.00

A simple and complete spray calendar is packed with each gun.

B. D. SHAKER

For applying dry insecticides, such as Bug Death, Slug Shot, Paris Green, etc.; made of tin; practical and durable. P. P. weight, 3 lbs., 75c.

PARIS GREEN SHAKERS

Tin. For dusting vegetables, potatoes, small fruits and shrubbery, 65c. each. P. P. weight, 2 lbs.

Farmers' Favorite. (See cut.) Large double-action affair, $4.00 each. P. P. weight, 4 lbs.

DICKEY DUSTER

Excellent for distributing Bug Death, Slug Shot, etc. Price, 60c. P. P. weight, 1 lb.

CHAMPION GUN

This machine will distribute dry insecticides, covering one or two rows at one time. Will save its price in material used in one season.
Price, $12.00.   P. P. weight, 8 lbs.

WOODASON HAND BELLOWS

	P. P. Wt.	
Large double cone; each	5 lbs.	$6.50
Large single cone; each	3 lbs.	4.50
Small single cone; each	2 lbs.	3.00
Liquid spraying; small	3 lbs.	3.75
Liquid spraying; large	4 lbs.	4.50
Sulphur Bellows; each		3.75

WHIRLWIND POWDER GUNS

For distributing dry powder. Price, 35c.
P. P. Weight, 8 oz.

OIL TORCHES

For burning out worms, caterpillars and tree pests.
P. P. Wt. Each
Reservoir, ½ lb. $0.50
Asbestos, 1 lb. .65

POLES FOR TORCHES, ETC.

Reservoir Torch   Asbestos Torch
Hardwood, 12 feet, $2.00; 14 feet, heavy, $2.25. Poles are not mailable.
Bamboo Poles. For brushing worm casts off putting greens, etc.

	Each	Doz.	100
14 ft.	$0.45	$4.75	$32.50
20 ft.	.65	7.00	55.00

AUTOMATIC COMPRESSED AIR SPRAYER

Parcel Post Weight, 2 lbs.
This is the grandest hand sprayer ever offered, very easily operated, especially desirable for ladies' use.
Tin.....each, $1.25 | Brass....each, $2.25

CYCLONE HAND SPRAYERS

Similar to the automatic, except they do not have the automatic air reservoir attachment. P. P. weight, 1½ lbs.
No. 112, Tin, large, 60c.; Midget Tin, small, 35c. No. 114, Brass, $1.25.

BUCKET SPRAY PUMP

These are made entirely of brass, except the foot rest and hand grip. The prices below do not include bucket, but include 3½ feet of ⅜-in. hose and nozzle.

No. 256. Success (without bucket fastener), $8.00. P. P. Wt., 7 lbs.
No. 689. Perfect Success (with bucket fastener), $8.50. P. P. Weight, 9 lbs.

Success Pump

No. 22 BINKS COMPRESSED AIR SPRAYER

Galvanized steel tank, 5 gals. capacity. Brass pump with a patent clamping device, equipped with 3 feet of hose, spray nozzle, shut-off cock and shoulder strap. P. P. Wt., 15 lbs. Price, $8.50.

No. 327½ Myers' Bucket Pump

This is a double brass chamber arrangement, and fills the want of those desiring a medium-priced sprayer. Price, $6.50. P. P. weight, 9 lbs.

No. 3 Paragon Sprayer

THE PARAGON SPRAYER

Especially desirable for the reason that it is not necessary to strain the material before pouring it into the reservoir, although we recommend that this be done; guaranteed to give absolute satisfaction. Excellent for applying whitewash or paint.
No. 0. Capacity, 3 gallons; equipped with 4 ft. hose, one 3-ft. extension pipe and 2 spray nozzles. Price, $15.00.
No. 1. With a 5-gal. reservoir, 5 ft. of hose and 2 extension pipes, $19.00.
No. 3. Equipped with a 12-gal. tank mounted on a truck, three 2½-ft. extension pipes, 2 nozzles and 10 ft. of hose, $26.00.
No. 4. Mounted on a two-wheel truck; equipped with 10 ft. of extension pipe, 20 ft. of hose and 2 nozzles. 25-gal. barrel, complete, $33.00.
Bucket Washers for Paragon Sprayers, 35c. each.

GOULD SPRAY PUMPS

This make of spray pump has been favorably regarded among gardeners, farmers and fruit growers for years.

GOULD'S MONARCH

2-Cylinder Hand Power Pump (Fig. 1506). This equipment is designed to be mounted on a platform for stationary use or for transportation on a wagon, sled or other means; it is probably the best of its class and is a pump that will last a lifetime with reasonable care. Plain Pump, No. O, price, $50.60.

Outfit C—Equipped with 5-ft. suction hose and strainer and 1 lead 15 ft. ½ in. special spray hose and 1 Mistry Jr. Nozzle. Price, $62.50.

Outfit D—Same as Outfit C, except the equipment is 2 leads of hose and 2 nozzles. Price, $70.85.

Pomona. No. 1100. Plain barrel pump. $29.70.

Pomona. No. 1100. Outfit C, with agitator, 15 ft. ½ in. special spray hose and 1 Mistry Jr. Nozzle. $38.15.

Pomona. No. 1100. Outfit D, with agitator and 2 15-ft. leads of special ½-in. spray hose and 2 Mistry Jr. Nozzles Price, $46.60.

Gould's Fruitall. Fig. 1188. Plain barrel pump. $16.20.

Gould's Fruitall. Fig. 1188 (Outfit C), with agitator and 1 15-ft. lead of ½-in. special spray hose and 1 Mistry Jr. Nozzle. $22.00.

Gould's Fruitall. Fig. 1188 (Outfit D), with agitator and 2 15-ft. leads of ½-in. special spray hose and 2 Mistry Jr. Nozzles. $27.80.

Gould's Standard. Fig. 905½. Plain barrel Pump. $24.00.

Gould's Standard. Fig. 905½ (Outfit C), without agitator, but with strainer and 1 15-ft. lead special spray hose and 1 Mistry Jr. Nozzle. $30.35.

Gould's Standard. Fig. 905½ (Outfit D), same as Outfit C, but equipped with 2 15-ft. leads of hose and 2 nozzles. Price, $38.80.

Bordeaux Nozzle　　**Vermorel Nozzle**

SPRAY NOZZLES (⅜ in. thread)

	P. P. Wt.	
Bordeaux and Vermorel	8 ozs.	$0.85
Mistry Jr.	5 ozs.	1.35
Paragon style	4 ozs.	.40
Duplex Vermorel (2 nozzles)	14 ozs.	2.25
Triple Vermorel (3 nozzles)	16 ozs.	3.10
Quadruple Vermorel (4 nozzles)	2 lbs.	4.00
Duplex Mistry (2 nozzles)	2 lbs.	3.20

For ¾-in. connections add 50c. to the above nozzle prices.

THE ROBERTSON POTATO SPRAYER

This is probably the first successful hand sprayer that distributes in a systematic fashion a spray solution on the top and underneath the foliage of potato vines and other plants. It is made of galvanized iron, in a substantial manner, and the reservoir is of liberal size; it may be used for general spraying in the vegetable and flower garden as well as elsewhere. Price, $1.50.

THE KIRKE FEEDER

Made to accommodate cartridges of various kinds, containing fertilizer and insecticide ingredients, each separate as below.

	Each.	Doz.
Nickeled Cartridge Holder	$3.00	
Angle Worm Cartridges	.80	$9.00
Nicotine Cartridges	.35	3.75
Salt Cartridges	.15	1.20
Arsenate of Lead Cartridges	.50	5.75
Fertilizer Cartridges	.20	2.00
Bordeaux Cartridges	.35	3.75

HEAVY BRASS SYRINGES

			Parcel Post.		
No.	Diam.	Length		Wt.	Price.
99	1½ in.	18 in.	1 spray	1¾ lbs.	$4.20
101	1¼ "	14 "	2 sprays	2 "	4.50
101A	1½ "	16 "	2 "	2¼ "	5.00
110	1¾ "	20 "	2 "	4½ "	9.00
120	1¾ "	20 "	Adjustable 5 "	11.00

EXTENSION PIPES, ETC.

For reaching into trees; ⅜-inch threads.
Bamboo, lined, 10 ft. $6.50
Galv. Iron, 2 ft., P. P. weight, 6 ozs. .45
Brass, 2 ft., P. P. weight, 8 ozs. .60
Pet Cock, for extension pipes .... .75
Paragon Extensions, 2½ ft., 50c. each.
Parcel post weight, 12 ozs.

THE AUTO-SPRAY

It operates with compressed air. Safe and efficient. Liquid capacity, 4 gallons; pressure capacity, 40 lbs. The Brown Auto-Spray is probably the first real successful compressed air sprayer ever put on the market. Previous to its introduction there were other makes, some of them still being offered for sale. We have had a wide and varied experience with the different ones, and after personal tests and noting the

Auto-Spray in Operation

experiences of our customers, finally adopted this make. They will successfully spray bushes, shrubbery and trees, the latter with the use of extension pipes. The brass tank sprayer is the best, as corrosive solutions can be used in it without injuring the same. Auto-Sprayers can be sent via parcels post; weight, 16 lbs.

No. 1-B. Brass. Equipped with hose and Auto-Pop Attachment, $11.00.

No. 1-D. Galvanized Iron. Equipped with hose and Auto-Pop, $7.50.

Auto-Pop Nozzle Attachment controls the flow instantly by a pressure of the hand. When Auto-Pop Attachment is purchased separately, $1.50 each, without hose; with hose, $2.00. P. P. Weight, 1 lb.

COPPER STRAINER

For straining whitewash, spraying material, etc. The neck is of the correct size to fit into the reservoir of an auto-spray, which allows both hands to be free when using it. $1.50 each. P. P. Weight, ¾ lb.

FLOWER BED FENCING

For putting around beds, lawns, etc.
Any length desired up to 150 running ft.
16 in. Less than 150 ft. roll, 20c. per ft.
16 in. In roll lots, 150 ft., 16c. per ft.
22 in. Less than 150 ft. roll, 25c. per ft.
22 in. In roll lots, 150 ft., 19c. per ft.

Continuous Wire Trellis.

Excellent for training vines of all kinds up porch-verandas, pergolas, etc. Thoroughly galvanized and well made.

Any length desired up to 150 running feet.
13 in. wide, less than 150 ft. rolls, 20c. per ft.
13 in. wide, in roll lots, 150 ft., 16c.
19 in. wide, less than 150 ft. rolls, 25c. per ft.
19 in. wide, in roll lots, 150 ft., 19c. per ft.

CARNATION SUPPORTS

The Richmond, shown below, is the most popular support on the market. Can be put together in minute and is always satisfactory; 29 in. high.

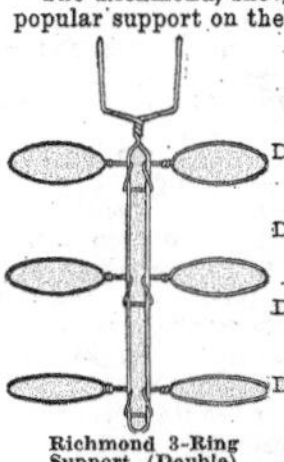

	Richmond, double		
	Doz.	100	1,000
	$1.25	$7.75	$70.00
	Richmond, single		
	Doz.	100	1,000
	$1.00	$6.50	$60.00
	Model, 2-ring		
	Doz.	100	1,000
	$1.00	$6.50	$55.00
	Model, 3-ring		
	Doz.	100	1,000
	$1.25	$7.00	$60.00

Richmond 3-Ring
Support (Double)

RUBBER SPRINKLERS

Either Straight Neck or Crook Neck
Spraywell, 6-oz. cap. Wt. 8 ozs.,.....$0.85
    8-oz. cap. Wt. 1 lb....... 1.00
Scollay No. 1. Wt. 1 lb.............. 1.50

GATHERING BASKET

Very convenient for carrying berry boxes, asparagus and other vegetables. Made of oak; 12 in. wide, 23 in. long, 4 in. deep. Price, $1.25.

GARDEN BASKETS

	No. 2, Stiff Handle	
		Each
½ Bu.	....	$1.00
	No. 3, Drop Handle	Each
½ Bu.	....	$1.00
	No. 4, Without Handle	Each
½ Bu.	....	$1.00
1 Bu.	....	1.25

TREE LABELS

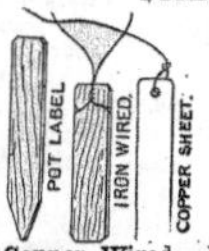

Parcel Post Weight, ½ lb. per 100.
Iron Wired.

		100	1000
Plain	......	$0.40	$2.35
Iron Wired.			
Painted	..	.50	2.75
Copper			
Wired. Plain	.30	2.00
Copper Wired.	Painted......	.40	2.35
Copper Sheet, wired...30c. doz.;	100,	1.75
Zinc Sheet, wired....30c. doz.;	100,	1.75
Indelible Marking Pencils.......each,		15c

PAINTED POT LABELS

	P. P. Wt.		
		100	1000
4 inch	.... ½ lb.	$0.30	$2.00
4½ inch	.... ½ lb.	.35	2.25
5 inch	.... ½ lb.	.40	2.45
6 inch	.... ¾ lb.	.50	3.00
8 inch	.........2 lbs.	1.40	8.50
10 inch	.........2½ lbs.	1.90	11.50
12 inch	.........3 lbs.	2.25	13.65
18 inch, for field use, 7 lbs.		3.25	30.00

GROWN WITH BAG   WITHOUT

GRAPE PROTECTING BAGS

Thousands of bunches of grapes are wasted annually because they are not protected against the ravages of insects, birds, etc. Michell's Improved Grape Bags are economical; easily attached and last a season. The fruit ripens just as readily in them as it does in the open. The bags should be attached when the grapes are the size of a pea prior to which it is suggested that they be sprayed (even though not affected) against blight or fungus, the bags should be left attached until the fruit is ready to harvest.

If desired by mail please add to the prices below as noted.

	Weight for mail per 100	100	1000
2 lb. size........1½ lbs.		$0.55	$5.00
3 lb. size........1½ lbs.		.65	5.50
4 lb. size........1½ lbs.		.70	6.00

SHADING OR PROTECTING CLOTH

Largely used as a substitute for glass where protection is desired. It is admirable for summer use, protecting plants, etc., from the sun and at the same time allowing ventilation.

	Yds. per Pc.	Per Yd.	Per Pc.
Light. Brown cloth...60		$0.25	$13.20
Medium. Brown cloth.60		.38	21.00
Heavy. Brown cloth..40		.50	18.00

SUNDRIES

Bulb Fibre. Qt., 15c.; 30c. ½ peck; peck, 50c.; 85c. ½ bu.; bu., $1.50.
Bull Dog Clips. For fastening packages, etc., $1.25 per box.
Carnation Clips (Baurs), for mending carnations. $1.00 per 1000.
Carnation Bands (Rubber). For mending bursted calyx. 30c. per oz.; ¼ lb., $1.00.
Carnation Staples (Wire). 60c. per 1000.
Charcoal, Lump. For use in potting. Pk., 50c.; $1.50 per bu.; barrel sack, $2.50.
Cocoanut Fibre. 10c. qt.; 4 qts., 30c.; 50c. peck; bushel, $1.50; $5.00 for 5 bushels.
Cork for Orchids, 50c. per lb.; 10 lbs., $4.00.
Glass Cleaner. $2.00 gal.; 5 gals., $9.50.
Grafting Wax. ¼ lb., 20c.; 30c. per ½ lb.; lb., 50c.; $2.40 for 5 lbs.
Moss (Green-Lump). Pk., 60c.; $1.50 per bu.; bbl. bag, $3.00. Green Sheet. ½ peck, 40c.; 70c. per peck; bu., $2.00; $3.50 per bbl. sack. Sphagnum (dry). Bbl. bales, $1.50; 5 bbl. bales, $4.50. Sphagnum (live). Pk., 40c.; $1.25 per bu.; bbl., $3.00.
Pebbles. Qt., 10c.; 60c. per pk.; bu., $1.75; $4.00 per bbl.
Peat or Leaf Mould. Pk., 40c.; $1.25 per bu.; bbl., $3.00.
Peat, Orchid. Pk., 40c.; $1.25 per bu.; bbl. bag, $3.00.
Pruning Compound. Per qt., 85c.; $2.25 per gal.
Sand. For propagating. Per qt., 10c.; 30c. per pk.; bu., $1.00; $3.00 per bbl.
Shaderine. For shading greenhouse glass. 5 lbs., $1.25; 10-lb. cans, $2.50.
Soil. For potting. Qt., 10c.; 20c. per ½ pk.; pk., 30c.; $1.00 per bu.; bbl., $3.00.
Toothpicks. Plain, box, 7c.; 35c. for 6.
Toothpicks. Wired, 45c. 1000; 10,000, $3.50.
Toothpicks. 6-inch, wired, green; per 375, 30c.; $2.00 per 3000.
Tree Paint (Target Brand). Qt., 85c.; $2.25 per gal.
Tin Foil. In 5- and 6-inch widths, in 1-lb. pkgs. and in 5-lb. rolls, 5-in. wide. 35c. per lb.; 5 lbs. for $1.50.
Violet and Green Foil. 60c. per lb.
Weed Killer. Michell's. Qt., 55c.; 90c. per ½ gal.; gal., $1.75; $6.75 per 5 gals.; 30 gals., $33.00; $50.00 for 50 gals.
Weed Killer. Herbicide. 60c. qt.; gal., $1.75; $7.00 per 5 gals.
Fairmount Weed Killer. ½ gal., 90c.; $1.50 per gal.; 5 gals., $6.25; $11.50 per 10 gals.; 50-gal. barrel, $45.00.
Zementine. For whitewashing and shading. 2 lbs., 35c.; $1.45 per 10 lbs.
Zinco. For destroying soot and its effects. 60c. per pkg.

All Prices Subject to Market Changes

(oe)

Alphano Inoculant. A soil bacteria to use in connection with growing legumes. 1 -acre size, net wt., 2 lbs., $1.00; 10-acre size, net wt., 20 lbs., $8.00.

Ashes (Hard Wood). Apply 1000 lbs. per acre. For top dressing lawn and grass fields, in early spring or late fall. 25 lbs., 85c.; $1.50 per 50 lbs.; 100 lbs., $2.50; $4.50 per 200-lb. sack; 1,000 lbs., $20.00; $37.50 per ton.

Asparagus Fertilizer (Michell's). A mixture that promotes the root and top growth. Apply 800 lbs. per acre. 25 lbs. for $1.25; $2.00 for 50 lbs.; 100 lbs. for $3.75; $6.50 for 200 lbs.; ton, $55.00.

Bon Arbor. A concentrated chemical fertilizer; used in liquid form. Per 8 oz., 30c.; 60c. per lb.; 5 lbs., $2.75.

Blood (Dried). For indoor culture of flowering plants, like roses, carnations, etc., its chief element being nitrogen. 5 lbs., 75c.; $1.25 per 10 lbs.; 25 lbs., $2.75; $5.00 per 50 lbs.; 100 lbs., $9.00; $17.50 per 200 lbs.

Bone Flour. Apply 600 lbs. per acre. Very fine, effective almost immediately; can be used for indoor or outdoor purposes. 25 lbs., $1.50; $2.75 per 50 lbs.; 100 lbs., $5.00; $9.50 per 200 lbs.

Bone Meal (Michell's Special Grade). Unusually rich in nitrogen and phosphoric acid, the two principal plant foods. We recommend this especially for lawns, gardens and greenhouses, or any purpose where a high-class fertilizer counts. Apply 800 to 1000 lbs. per acre. 3 lbs., 25c.; 35c. for 5 lbs.; 10 lbs., 60c.; $1.35 for 25 lbs.; 50 lbs., $2.50; $4.50 per 100 lbs.; 200 lbs., $8.50; $38.50 per ½ ton; ton, $75.00.

Chrysanthemum Manure (Thomson's Special). Especially recommended and used by the leading private gardeners of England and America. Per 28-lb. sack, $4.00; $8.00 per 56-lb. sack.

Clay's Fertilizer. An English chemical fertilizer, for forcing greenhouse plants and vegetables. It can be used in either dry or liquid form. 28 lbs., $3.50; $9.50 for 56 lbs.; 112 lbs., $14.00.

Climax Lawn Sand. An unique combination of carefully dried and finely ground chemicals. Destroys weeds in lawns. 3½-lb. can, 60c.; $1.10 per 7-lb. can; 14-lb. can, $1.75; $3.00 per 28-lb. pkg.; 56-lb. pkg., $4.75; $9.25 for 112 lbs.

Cotton Seed Meal. Apply 800 lbs. per acre. Exceedingly rich in potash and ammonia, making it excellent for use as a grass and grain fertilizer. Price on application.

Cow or Cattle Manure (Shredded). Convenient to handle, making it possible for everyone to get this usually scarce article at all times. Apply 1000 lbs. per acre. $3.50 per 100 lbs.; 500 lbs., $16.25; $27.50 per 1000 lbs.; ton, $54.00.

Hay and Pasture Grass Fertilizer (Michell's). A splendid mixture for top dressing wheat, rye, timothy and grass fields. Apply 800 to 1000 lbs. per acre. 25 lbs. for $1.00; $1.75 for 50 lbs.; 100 lbs., $3.25; 200 lbs. for $6.00; $27.50 per 1000 lbs.; per ton, $52.50.

Hog Manure (Pulverized). Put up and sold in 100-lb. bags only; splendid for forcing vegetables and flowering plants, increasing size and yield. Per 100 lbs., $3.50; $16.25 for 500 lbs.

Horn Shavings. Used principally for mixing in potting; especially valuable in chrysanthemum growing. 5 lbs., 75c.; $1.20 for 10 lbs.; 25 lbs., $2.25; $4.00 for 50 lbs.; 100 lbs., $7.00.

Humus (Alphano Prepared). An excellent article to incorporate with poor soil in the garden, greenhouse or in potting plants. When used in garden work, the ground should be covered with ½ to 2 inches of Humus and spaded in. 5 lbs., 35c.; 60c. for 10 lbs.; 25 lbs. for 90c.; $2.75 per 100 lbs.; 500 lbs., $12.00; $18.00 per 1000 lbs.; 2000 lbs., $32.50. (Special price f. o. b. Alphano, N. J.)

Kainit. For top dressing; asparagus beds, etc. Price on application.

Land Plaster. Used for top dressing newly plowed land prior to harrowing; also for sweetening the soil on lawns and fields. Apply 1500 to 2000 lbs. per acre. 40c. for 10 lbs.; 25 lbs., 60c.; $1.00 for 50 lbs.; 100 lbs., 1.75; $3.25 for 200 lbs.; ton, $25.00.

Lime (Hydrated or Powdered). Promotes growth and gives the grass a rich color. Apply one ton per acre. Per 125-lb. sack, $2.50; $9.00 per 500 lbs.; 1000 lbs., $16.00; $30.00 per ton.

Limestone (Pulverized). For applying on sour or wornout soils at the rate of 1 ton per acre. Put up in 100-lb. bags, $1.75 per bag; 500 lbs., $6.50; $11.00 per 1000 lbs.; ton, $20.00.

Limoid. Made from pure lump lime, thoroughly hydrated. 10-lb. pkg., 40c.

Manure (Fresh Horse, Stockyard and Cow). At short notice we can usually supply first-class horse, cow and stockyard manure in carload lots only. Prices on request.

Mulford's Culture. For inoculating Clovers and other legumes. When ordering, please state for what crop you desire to use it. Trial size for beans and peas, 25c. Garden size (¼ acre), 50c.; 1-acre size, $1.50; 5-acre size, $5.00.

Muriate of Potash. Apply 100 to 150 lbs. per acre, usually with other fertilizers. Excellent for potatoes, corn, grains, etc. Analysis, equal to 50 per cent. actual potash. 5 lbs., $1.25; $2.00 per 10 lbs.; 25 lbs., $4.00; $12.00 per 100 lbs.

Nitrate of Soda. Apply 100 to 150 lbs. per acre, mixing with land plaster or other fertilizers to render application more easy. Use only after plants are above ground. If used in liquid form dilute 2 ozs. to 1 gal. of water and do not apply oftener than twice a week. 1 lb., 20c.; 75c. for 5 lbs.; 10 lbs., $1.30; $2.50 per 25-lb. bag; 50-lb. bag, $4.25; $8.00 per 100 lbs.

Phosphate for Corn (Michell's). Apply 800 lbs. per acre. This contains the necessary ingredients to produce a bumper crop of corn. 25 lbs. for $1.00; $1.75 for 50 lbs.; 100 lbs. for $3.25; $5.50 for 200 lbs.; per ½ ton, $26.00; $50.00 per ton.

Phosphate, High-Grade Acid Tennessee or South Carolina Rock. 14 per cent. Apply 1000 lbs. per acre. Used for mixing with other fertilizers to increase the phosphoric acid analysis. In 200-lb. sacks only, $5.00; $21.00 per ½ ton; per ton, $40.00.

Phosphate, Michell's High-Grade Ammoniated. For all vegetable crops, grains, grass, etc. Apply 800 to 1000 lbs. per acre broadcast. 5 lbs., 35c.; 60c. per 10 lbs.; 25 lbs., $1.25; $2.00 per 50 lbs.; 100 lbs., $3.50; $6.50 per 200 lbs.; ton, $57.50.

Plant Food. A highly concentrated chemical fertilizer for house use. Michell's, 20c. per 6-oz. pkg. Bowker's, 4-oz. pkgs., 25c.; 35c. per 12-oz. pkg. Allow for postage if wanted by mail.

Plant Life (Zenke's). A liquid plant food, tonic and fertilizer. Per 8 oz., 25c.; 90c. per qt.; ½ gal., $1.65; $3.25 per gal.

Potato Manure (Michell's). Apply at the rate of from 800 to 1000 lbs. per acre. 25 lbs., $1.50; $2.25 per 50 lbs.; per 100 lbs., $3.75; $7.00 per 200 lbs.; per ½ ton, $32.50; $62.50 per ton.

Poudrette (Native Guano). Apply 1000 lbs. per acre. Extensively used for garden, lawns, in making compost and in fact wherever a good, quick acting fertilizer is wanted. 25 lbs., $1.25; $1.75 per 50 lbs.; 100 lbs., $2.75; $4.25 per 200 lbs.; 1000 lbs., $20.00; $35.00 per ton.

Salt. For asparagus beds and putting on walks and roads to kill weeds. Apply 800 lbs. per acre in early spring. 25 lbs. for 75c.; $1.25 for 50 lbs.; $2.00 per 100 lbs.; 200 lbs., $3.50; $30.00 per ton.

Sheep Manure (Wizard Brand). Apply 1000 lbs. per acre. For garden, lawn or greenhouse use. 2 lbs., 20c.; 35c. per 5 lbs.; 10 lbs., 60c.; $1.00 per 25 lbs.; 50 lbs., $1.75; $3.50 per 100 lbs.; 500 lbs., $16.25; $27.50 per 1000 lbs.; per ton, $54.00.

Soot (Imported Scotch). This is used principally for bringing a good healthy color into the foliage of chrysanthemum and other greenhouse plants. Price on application.

Sulphate of Ammonia. Apply 75 to 100 lbs. per acre only with other fertilizers deficient in nitrogen. Price on application.

Sulphate of Potash. Apply 100 to 125 lbs. per acre, usually with other fertilizers. Price on application.

Tankage. For roses, etc., under glass; similar to dried blood. $2.00 per 50 lbs.; 100 lbs., $3.75; $6.50 per 200 lbs.; ton, $60.00.

Thomson's Special Flower, Vegetable and Vine Manure is extensively used wherever it is desired to force flowers or vegetables. 28 lbs., $3.00; $5.75 per 56 lbs.; 112 lbs., $10.00.

Tobacco Stems. For fumigating, mulching and fertilizing; an excellent top dressing for lawns in winter. 40c. for 5 lbs.; $1.00 per bu.; per bbl. sack, $1.75; in large bales, at 2½c. per lb.; $17.00 per ½ ton; per ton, $32.00.

Wheat Fertilizer (Michell's). For grass and grain crops. Apply 800 lbs. per acre. 25 lbs. for $1.10; $1.75 for 50 lbs.; 100 lbs., $3.00; $5.00 for 200 lbs.; ½ ton, $23.75; $45.00 per ton.

PLEASE NOTE—No smaller quantity of a kind of fertilizer than offered can be supplied (08)

Michell's Insect Destroyers, Etc.

DIRECTIONS FOR USING ANY OF THE FOLLOWING WILL BE FOUND ON EACH PACKAGE, OR WE SHALL BE PLEASED TO GIVE INFORMATION BY MAIL OR OTHERWISE.

Ant Exterminator (Magic). Per ¼ lb., 20c.; 40c. per ½ lb.; lb., 75c.; $3.00 per 5 lbs.

Ant Exterminator (Zenke's). An effective liquid form of this important insecticide. 8 oz., 25c.; 85c. per qt.; ½ gal., $1.75; $3.50 per gal.

Aphine, ¼ pt., 25c.; 40c. per ½ pt.; per pt., 65c.; $1.00 per qt.; gal., $3.00.

Aphis Punk. Per pkg., 85c.; $7.00 per 12 pkgs.

Arsenate of Lead (Paste). Per lb., 40c.; $1.65 per 5 lbs.; 10 lbs., $3.00; per 25 lbs., $6.00; 50 lbs., $10.50; $19.50 per 100 lbs.

Arsenate of Lead (Powdered). Per lb., 55c.; $2.65 per 5 lbs.; 10 lbs., $5.00; $10.50 per 25 lbs.; 50 lbs., $20.00; $37.50 per 100 lbs.

Black Leaf 40. Per 1-oz. bottle, 25c.; $1.00 per ½ lb.; 2 lbs., $3.25; $13.75 per 10 lbs.

Bordeaux Arsenate. Per lb., 40c.; $1.50 per 5 lbs.; 10 lbs., $2.75; $6.00 per 25 lbs.; 50 lbs., $10.00; $18.50 per 100 lbs.

Bordeaux Mixture (Dry Form). Per lb., 30c.; $1.25 per 5 lbs.; 10 lbs., $2.00.

Bordeaux Mixture (Paste Form). This we offer in 5-gal. kegs only. Price, $7.25.

Boro Wax. Per qt., 40c.; 75c. per ½ gal.; gal., $1.25.

Bug Death. Per lb., 20c.; 50c. per 3 lbs.; 5 lbs., 75c.; $1.65 per 12½ lbs.; 100 lbs., $8.50.

Bug Death. For destroying aphis on vegetable plants. Per 12-oz. pkg., 20c.; $8.50 for 80 lbs.

Carbolineum (Arvenarius). (Now called Protexol.) Per gal., $1.50; $7.00 per 5 gals.

Copper Solution. Per qt., $1.25; $3.50 per gal.

Cyanegg. For making hydrocyanic acid gas. Per lb., 85c.

Dalmatian or Persian Powder. Per ¼ lb., 30c.; 55c. per ½ lb.; lb., 90c.; $4.00 per 5 lbs.

Fir Tree Oil Soap. Per ½ lb., 35c.; $1.00 per 2-lb. can.

Fish Oil Soap (Good's Caustic). Per lb., 35c.; $1.50 per 5 lbs.; 25 lbs., $5.50.

Fish Oil Soap. Per ½ lb., 15c.; 25c. per lb.; 5 lbs., $1.00; $1.80 per 10 lbs.; 25 lbs., $4.00; $11.00 per 100 lbs.

Fungicide (Zenke's). For various forms of fungus. Per 8 oz., 25c.; 85c. per qt.; ½ gal., $1.75; $3.50 per gal.

Fungine. Per ½ pt., 40c.; 65c. per pt.; qt., $1.00; $3.00 per gal.

Getz-There Soap. Per 2 lbs., 60c.; $1.75 per 8 lbs.; 50 lbs., $7.00.

Grape Dust. Per 5 lbs., $1.00; $1.85 per 10 lbs.

Hellebore. Per ¼ lb., 25c.; 40c. per ½ lb.; lb., 70c.; $3.00 per 5 lbs.

Imp Soap Spray. 65c. per pt.; per qt., 85c.; $2.75 per gallon; 5 gals., $12.00; $22.50 per 10 gallons.

Insecticide (Zenke's General Greenhouse). For the destruction and control of many pests. Per 8 oz., 25c.; 85c. per qt.; ½ gal., $1.00; $1.75 per gal.

IXL Compound. Per gal., $6.00; $27.50 for 5 gals.

Kerosene Emulsion (Liquid). 70c. per qt.; per gal., $1.75.

Lemon Oil Insecticide. Per ½ pt., 35c.; 60c. per pt.; qt., $1.00; $1.75 per ½ gal.; gal., $3.00; $12.00 per 5-gal. keg.

CARBONDALE HYDROMETERS

These are highly recommended by the Pennsylvania State Department of Agriculture for testing the gravity of Lime Sulphur solution. One should be in the hands of every man who uses this material. Price, $1.25. (Postpaid, $1.35.) With directions.

Lime Sulphur. Per qt., 45c.; 75c. per ½ gal.; gal., $1.25; $4.00 per 5 gals.; 30-gal. bbls., 35c. gal.; 50-gal. bbls., 30c. gal.

Lime Sulphur (Dry Powder Form). Per lb., 35c.; $1.50 per 5 lbs.; 10 lbs., $2.00; $4.00 per 25 lbs.; 100 lbs., $12.50.

Mo Lo. A preparation for ridding gardens and lawns of moles and field mice. Pkg., 25c.

Nico-Fume (Liquid). ¼ lb., 65c.; $2.00 per lb.; 4 lbs., $7.50; $14.50 per 8 lbs.

Nico-Fume Paper. Per box, 24 sheets, $1.25; $5.00 per 144 sheets; 288 sheets, $9.50.

Nikoteen. Per oz., 40c.; 60c. per 1¾ oz.; 8 oz., $1.25; $2.25 per pt., per ½ gal. (4 lbs.), $7.50; per gal. (8 lbs.), $13.50.

Paris Green. Per ¼ lb., 20c.; 35c. per ½ lb.; lb., 60c.; $1.20 per 2 lbs.; 5 lbs., $2.90; $7.60 per 14 lbs.

Protexol (See Carbolineum). For preserving wood, etc.

Pyrox (Bowker's). Per lb., 45c.; $1.75 per 5 lbs.; 10 lbs., $3.00; $6.25 per 25 lbs.; 50 lbs., $11.00; $20.00 per 100 lbs.; 300 lbs., $57.00.

Rat Corn. For destroying rats and mice. 25c., 50c. and $1.00 per box.

Readeana Rose Bug Exterminator. Trial bottle, 30c.; 50c. per 8 ozs.; 24 ozs., $1.00; $4.00 per gal.

Scalecide. Per qt., 70c.; $1.85 per gal.; 5 gals., $7.25; $12.50 per 10 gals.; 30-gal. bbl., $31.00; $46.00 per 50 gal.

Scale Destroyer (Soluble Oil). Qt., 60c.; 85c. per ½ gal.; gal., $1.50; $6.25 per 5 gals.

Shoo Fly. Per qt., 45c.; $1.25 per gal.

Slug Shot. Per lb. canister, 20c.; 60c. per 5 lbs.; 10 lbs., $1.00; $2.35 per 25 lbs.; 100 lbs., $8.75. Barrel lots in bulk (250 lbs.), 8½c. lb.

Sulco-V. B. Will control San Jose and other scale insects, and many species of plant lice and fungus disease. Pt., 40c.; 75c. per qt.; ½ gal., $1.35; $2.50 per gal.; 5 gals., $8.50; $15.00 per 10 gals.; ½ bbl. (about 30 gals.), $1.00 per gal.; bbl. (about 50 gals.), 90c. per gal.

Sulphate of Copper. Per lb., 20c.; 90c. per 5 lbs.; $1.60 for 10 lbs.

Sulphur Candles. Large: 25c. each; per doz., $2.50. Small: 15c. each; per doz., $1.50.

Sulphur (Flowers). Per lb., 15c.; 60c. per 5 lbs.; 10 lbs., $1.15; $2.25 per 25 lbs.; 100 lbs., $8.00.

Sulpho Tobacco Soap. Per 3-oz. pkg., 15c.; 25c. per 6-oz. pkg.

Tobacco Dust (Special Dusting or Fumigating). 15c. per lb.; 5 lbs., 50c.; 90c. per 10 lbs.; 25 lbs., $2.00; $3.50 per 50 lbs.; 100 lbs., $6.00.

Tobacco Soap (Sulpho). 3 ozs., 15c.; 25c. per 6 ozs.

Tobacco Stems. Per lb., 15c.; 40c. per 5 lbs.; bushel, $1.00; $1.75 per bbl. sack; large bales at 2½c. per lb.; ½-ton, $17.00; $32.00 per ton.

Thrip Juice (Hammond's No. 2). Pt., 85c.; $1.50 per qt.; gal., $4.00.

Tree Tanglefoot. Per lb., 50c.; $1.45 per 3-lb. can.; 10 lbs., $4.50; $8.75 per 20 lbs.; 25 lbs., $10.50.

Vermine. A soil sterilizer and germicide; will destroy worms, maggots, etc. Per ¼ pt., 25c.; 40c. per ½ pt.; pt., 65c.; $1.00 per qt.; gal., $3.00.

Worm Destroyer (Michell's Brand). For using in gardens, on lawns, etc. (Price on application).

Worm Destroyer (Carter's Brand). F. o. b. Philadelphia: Per 100 lbs., $12.00; $110.00 per 1000 lbs.; ton, $210.00. F. o. b. Boston: Per 100 lbs., $10.50; $200.00 per ton.

Worm Eradicator (Reade's Electric). 8 ozs., 50c.; $1.00 per 24 ozs.; gal., $4.00.

Zenke's Insecticide (See Insecticide).

Zenoleum. ½ pt., 35c.; 75c. per qt.; ½ gal., $1.25; $2.00 per gal.; 5-gal. can, $9.50.

LAMPS for vaporizing nicotine solutions, 80c. each.

Price on all Insect Destroyers is Subject to Change (oe)

MICHELL'S FLOWER POTS, TUBS, ETC.

Orchid Pan · Earthen Fern Pan · Fern Dish Liner · Seed Pan · Wood Fibre Flower Vase

Cedar Tub · Keystone Tub · Earthen Flower Pot · Azalea Pot · Earthen Bulb Pan · Earthenware Saucer · Wood Fibre Saucer · Rolling Stand

CEDAR TUBS

Equipped with Strong Iron Handles

These are made by hand, of the very best white cedar painted green, bound with black iron hoops.

	Inside Diam.		Each
No. 0	24¾	in.	$15.00
No. 1	23⅜	"	13.35
No. 2	21⅜	"	11.90
No. 3	18 11-16	"	9.65
No. 4	16½	"	7.80
No. 5	14 7-16	"	7.05
No. 6	12 7-16	"	5.60
No. 7	11¾	"	4.95
No. 8	10 11-16	"	4.30

MICHELL'S KEYSTONE PLANT TUBS

Made of white cedar, painted green and bound with strong electric welded wire hoops, which do not rust. Handles are sold separately at 25c. per pair, not attached to tub.

	Inside Diam.	Depth	Each
No. 1	6 in.	6 in.	$0.85
No. 2	7 "	7 "	.90
No. 3	8 "	8 "	.95
No. 4	9 "	9 "	1.00
No. 5	10 "	9 "	1.20
No. 6	11 "	10 "	1.45
No. 7	12 "	11 "	1.75
No. 8	13 "	12 "	2.25
No. 9	14 "	13 "	2.55
No. 10	15 "	14 "	2.80
No. 11	16 "	15 "	3.15
No. 12	17 "	16 "	3.70
No. 13	18 "	17 "	4.50
No. 14	19 "	18 "	5.35

ROLLING STANDS for Tubs, Pots, etc.

In.	Weight	Will fit Pot	Will fit Tub	Each
12 in.	2 lbs.	10 in.		$1.35
14 "	2½ lbs.	12 "	No. 8	1.60
16 "	3 lbs.	14 "	" 8	2.50
18 "	3½ lbs.	16 "	" 7-6	3.00
20 "			" 5	3,25
22 "			" 4	3.50

PAPER FLOWER POTS

Ins. Diam.	Parcel Post Weight per doz.	Parcel Post Weight per 100	per doz.	100	1000
2¼	3 ozs.	2 lbs.	$0.15	$0.80	$5.08
2½	3 "	2 "	.20	.95	5.80
3	5 "	2 "	.25	1.10	7.75
3½	7 "	3 "	.30	1.50	10.46
4	8 "	4 "	.35	1.65	12.70
5	15 "	7 "	.50	2.75	20.02
6	2 lbs.	11 "	.60	3.30	26.98

AZALEA POTS

Diam.	Depth	Each	Doz.	100
5 in.	4½ in.	$0.09	$0.87	$5.76
6 "	5 "	.14	1.30	8.64
7 "	6 "	.23	2.16	14.40
8 "	7 "	.33	3.12	20.80
9 "	7½ "	.50	4.80	32.00
10 "	8 "	.68	6.48	43.20
12 "	10 "	1.38	13.20	88.00

FERN DISH LINERS

Very shallow, for inside of fancy silver or porcelain ferneries.

Width	Depth	Each	Doz.	100
7 in.	1⅞ in.	$0.22	$2.16	$14.40

SEED PANS (Earthenware)

	Each	Doz.
6 inches square	$1,25	$12.00
8 " "	1.68	16.08
10 " "	2.10	20.16
12 " "	2.50	24.00

EARTHEN BULB PANS

	Each	Doz.	100
6 inches diam.	$0.14	$1.30	$8.64
7 " "	.23	2.16	14.40
8 " "	.33	3.12	20.80
9 " "	.50	4.80	32.00
10 " "	.68	6.48	43.20
12 " "	1.38	13.20	88.00
14 " "	2.25	21.60	144.00

WOOD FIBRE FLOWER VASES

No.	Diam.	Depth	Weight	Each
0	8 in.	13 in.	4 lbs.	$2.25
1	5½ "	10 "	2½ "	2.00
2	4½ "	9 "	1½ "	1.80
3	4 "	6 "	1½ "	1.60
4	3 "	4½ "	¾ "	1.35
00	9 "	21 "	6 "	7.00
11	5 "	18 "	4 "	2.75
22	4½ "	15 "	2 "	3.00
33	4 "	12 "	2 "	2.25
44	3 "	9 "	1 "	2.00

VASES—Ideal Cut Flower

(Galvanized)

	Depth	Diam.	Each
No. 1	6½ in.	6 in.	$0.75
No. 2	9¼ "	8 "	.90
No. 3	9 "	7¾ "	.90
No. 4	12 "	9¼ "	1.10
No. 5	9 "	5½ "	.95
No. 6	11 "	7 "	1,00
No. 7	13¾ "	8¼ "	1.20
No. 8	19 "	7⅜ "	1.50

EARTHEN FLOWER POTS

Height and Width inside	Each	Doz.	100	1000
1 inch	$0.03	$0.22	$1.44	$13.50
2 "	.02	.18	1.20	11.25
2¼ "	.03	.21	1.36	12.75
2½ "	.03	24	1.60	15.00
3 "	.04	.32	2.08	19.50
3½ "	.04	.39	2.56	24.00
4 "	.05	.48	3.20	30.00
4½ "	.07	.65	4.32	40.50
5 "	.09	.87	5.76	54.00
5½ "	.12	1.08	7.20	67.50
6 "	.14	1.30	8.64	81.00
6½ "	.18	1.73	11.52	108.00
7 "	.23	2.16	14.40	......
8 "	.33	3.12	20.80	......
9 "	.50	4.80	32.00	......
10 "	.68	6.48	43.20	......
11 "	1.00	9.60	64.00	......
12 "	1.38	13.20	88.00	......
14 "	2.25	21.60	144.00	......

EUREKA POT HANGERS

15c. each; doz., $1.50; $10.00 per 100.

KRICK POT HANGERS

	Each	Doz.
No. 1	$0.05	$0.50
No. 2	.06	.60
No. 3	.07	.70

WOODEN ORCHID BASKETS

(Square)

	Each	Doz.
4 inch	$0.40	$4.50
10 "	.70	7.00
12 "	.80	9.00

ORCHID PANS (Round) (Earthen)

	Each	Doz
4 inches diam.	$0.20	$2.00
6 " "	.30	3.25
8 " "	.40	4.25
10 " "	.65	7.25
12 " "	1.00	11.00

EARTHEN FERN PANS

Width	Height	Each	Doz.	100
4 in.	1⅞ in.	$0.08	$0.72	$4.80
4¾ "	2⅛ "	.10	.96	6.40
5½ "	2¼ "	.13	1.20	8.00
6¼ "	2½ "	.15	1.44	9.60
7 "	2⅝ "	.18	1.68	11.20
8 "	3⅜ "	.25	2.40	16.00
9 "	3¼ "	.30	2.88	19.20

EARTHENWARE SAUCERS

	Each	Doz.	100
4 inches	$0.04	$0.36	$2.40
5 "	.05	.48	3.20
6 "	.08	.72	4.80
7 "	.10	.96	6.40
8 "	.14	1.32	8.80
9 "	.19	1.80	12.00
10 "	.22	2.16	14.40
11 "	.28	2.64	17.60
12 "	.34	3.24	21.60
14 "	.56	5.40	36.00

WOOD FIBRE SAUCERS

Extremely desirable on account of being absolutely waterproof.

	Parcel Post Weight Each	Each	Doz.
5 inches	¼ lb.	$0.50	$5.20
6 "	¼ "	.55	5.50
7 "	½ "	.60	6.00
8 "	½ "	.65	6.50
9 "	¾ "	.70	7.00
10 "	¾ "	.75	7.80
12 "	1¼ lbs.	.80	8.60
14 "	1½ "	1.10	11.20
16 "	2 "	1.75	19.80
18 "	2½ "	2.10	23.00
20 "	4 "	3.00	32.00

Larger sizes can be furnished as complete rolling stands only.

NOTE.—Earthenware cannot be packed for shipment by Parcel Post.

MICHELL'S LIQUID WEED KILLERS

An effective combination of high-grade chemicals which, diluted in water, destroys the roots as well as the tops of all weeds and vegetation to which it is applied.

One gallon diluted is sufficient to cover 100 to 125 square yards; and one or two applications are sufficient for an entire season. Does not injure marble, cement or fencing. The best time for applying is just after a rain.

PRICES OF MICHELL'S WEED KILLER

Per quart—makes 41 quarts.....$0.55   Per 5-gal. can, makes 205 gals. $6.75
Per ½ gallon—makes 20½ gals.. .90   Per 30-gal. can, makes 1230 gals. 33.00
Per gallon—makes 41 gals....... 1.75   Per 50-gal. can, makes 2050 gals. 50.00

HERBICIDE

This preparation is a thoroughly proven Weed Exterminator. Will not stain wood or stone work. It dilutes readily in water and can be applied with a sprinkling can or in a large area with a watering cart. For clay and sand tennis courts it is a perfect preparation. One part Herbicide dilutes to 40 parts of water, either hot or cold, clean or dirty. A gallon of Herbicide is capable of treating 120 square yards of surface.

PRICES OF HERBICIDE

	Price		Price
1 quart makes 41 quarts	$0.60	5 gallons makes 205 gallons	$7.00
½ gallon makes 20½ gallons...	1.00	25-gal. bbl. makes 1025 gallons..	27.50
1 gallon makes 41 gallons	1.75	50-gal. bbl. makes 2050 gallons..	50.00

FAIRMOUNT WEED KILLER

This is the original brand of liquid weed killer and is still in great demand; it is diluted and applied with a watering can, one gallon of material effectively treating about 125 square yards.

DILUTION			PRICE
½ gallon makes 25 gallons liquid	....	Per ½ gallon,	$0.90
1 gallon makes 50 gallons liquid	....	Per gallon,	1.50
5 gallons makes 250 gallons liquid	....	Per 5 gallons,	6.25
10 gallons makes 500 gallons liquid	....	Per 10 gallons,	11.50
50 gallons makes 2500 gallons liquid	....	Per 50-gal. bbl.,	45.00

MICHELL'S CLIMAX LAWN SAND

FOR USE ON LAWNS AND GRASS PLOTS

"Climax Lawn Sand" is a unique combination of finely ground chemicals, which, when sprinkled over the grass, possess the remarkable property of destroying Moss, Chickweed, Plantains, Dandelion, and all other weeds on Lawns, Tennis Courts, Golf Greens, etc., at the same time promoting the growth of the finer grasses.

"Climax Lawn Sand" may be applied any time during the growing season of the year, namely, from beginning of April to the end of October.

The lawn must be absolutely dry; by that is meant that no rain or dew must be visible on the grass.

Ten to twelve a. m. during the months of April, May and October, nine to twelve a. m. during June, July, August and September are the best hours for application.

Only apply in fine weather when the temperature is fairly high and when no rain appears likely for a day or two. This is most important.

After applying, the weeds blacken and die; the grass usually also becomes blackened and may remain so for a few days, but it quickly recovers its color, and young growths appear on the bare spots previously occupied by the weeds.

Should the weather be very hot and dry, the lawn should be thoroughly watered at the expiration of 48 hours after the application.

It acts as one of the most powerful fertilizers for grasses if applied as a top-dressing in the early spring. For top dressing as a fertilizer apply ¼ ton per acre.

QUANTITY REQUIRED AS A WEED DESTROYER

3½ lbs. will dress 150 square feet.	$0.60	
7 lbs. will dress 250 square feet.	1.10	Allow for
14 lbs. will dress 500 square feet.	1.75	Postage
28 lbs. will dress 1000 square feet.	3.00	if desired
56 lbs. will dress 2000 square feet.	4.75	by Mail
112 lbs. will dress 4000 square feet.	9.25	

MICHELL'S IMPROVED GRAPE BAGS

Thousands of bunches of grapes are wasted annually because they are not protected against the ravages of insects, birds, etc. Michell's Improved Grape Bags are economical, easily attached and last a season. The fruit ripens just as readily in them as it does in the open. The bags should be attached when the grapes are the size of a pea prior to which it is suggested that they be sprayed (even though not affected) against blight or fungus, the bags should be left attached until the fruit is ready to harvest.

If desired by mail please add to the prices below as noted.

	Weight for mail per 100	100	1000
2 lb. size ....1½ lbs.		$0.55	$5.00
3 lb. size ....1½ lbs.		.65	5.50
4 lb. size ....1½ lbs.		.70	6.00

ERADO WEED GUN

As handy as a cane, which it resembles. Fill the reservoir, which holds about 2 quarts of liquid, with Herbicide or Michell's Weed Killer, diluted. It will destroy weeds of all kinds in lawns without hurting the grass. Press the sharp point of the gun into the heart of the weed until the flat stay pieces touch the ground, when a quantity sufficient to kill is discharged into the heart of the plant which is destroyed for all time. Price, $1.25. Galvanized iron. (See cut.) Parcel Post weight, 2 lbs.

All Prices Subject to Change   **HENRY F. MICHELL CO., 516-518 MARKET STREET PHILADELPHIA**

CPSIA information can be obtained
at www.ICGtesting.com
Printed in the USA
LVHW021254071118
596294LV00004B/592